NATURAL DISASTERS OR SUPERNATURAL FORCES BEYOND MAN'S CONTROL?

They call it the *Jinx Sea*, the *Devil's Triangle*, the *Hoodoo Sea, Triangle of Death,* and *Port of the Missing*. Yet what is the truth about this seemingly ordinary area of the Atlantic Ocean —these waters which many have traveled through in complete safety but which have claimed a devastating toll of victims under the most uncanny circumstances? Thousands of people have been lost there, hundreds of ships and planes have disappeared never to be heard from again. Why? Where to? How?

Now at last a book unravels the mystery of these deadly waters to reveal the complete, sometimes startling, always frightening saga of

THE RIDDLE OF THE BERMUDA TRIANGLE

T5-CUR-510

THE RIDDLE OF THE BERMUDA TRIANGLE

EDITED BY

Martin Ebon

A SIGNET BOOK

NEW AMERICAN LIBRARY

TIMES MIRROR

ACKNOWLEDGMENTS

"World-Wide Seas of Mystery," by Ivan T. Sanderson, originally
appeared under the title "The 12 Devil's Graveyards Around the
World" in *Saga*, October, 1972. Copyright © 1972 by Gambi
Publications, Inc. Reprinted by permission.

"Jinxed Seas," by C. Winn Upchurch, originally appeared in the
U.S. Coast Guard Alumni Association *Bulletin*, July-August, 1960.
Copyright © 1960 by U.S. Coast Guard Alumni Association.
Reprinted by permission.

"The *Cyclops* Mystery," by Conrad A. Nervig, originally appeared
in the U.S. Naval Institute *Proceedings*, July, 1969. Copyright
© 1969 by United States Naval Institute. Reprinted by permission.

"Did the *Cyclops* Turn Turtle?" by Mahlon S. Tisdale, originally
appeared in the U.S. Naval Institute *Proceedings*, April, 1920.
Copyright 1920 by United States Naval Institute. Reprinted by
permission.

"Edgar Cayce and the Search for Atlantis," by David D. Zink, has
been adapted by its author from "The Search for Atlantis Continues: The 1974 Bimini Expedition of *Makai II*," which appeared
in *The ARE Journal*, May, 1975. Copyright © 1975 by The Association for Research and Enlightenment. Reprinted by permission.

FIRST PRINTING, JULY, 1975

3 4 5 6 7 8 9

PRINTED IN THE UNITED STATES OF AMERICA

The author wishes to express his appreciation for cooperation extended by various branches of the United States Coast Guard, notably in New York and Washington, D.C.

Contents

the control tower, "We cannot see land. Repeat. We cannot see land!" and was even unable to determine which direction was west. *page 25*

II. PIECES
OF THE RIDDLE

III. FANTASIES, GUESSES, AND CERTAINTIES

Based on a talk by the former lecturer in paranormal phenomena at Clark University, this analysis links the Bermuda Triangle mysteries with today's far-out world of physics, where "matter is more of an experience than a substance, things can exist in two or more places at the same time, or they can go from hither to yon without crossing the space in between, and time itself can run backward." *page 107*

IV. APPENDIX

provide the reader with a representative example of a thorough naval investigation, the full text of the U.S. Coast Guard's report on the disappearance of the *Marine Sulphur Queen*, in February 1963, is provided in this section. It offers details on the construction and performance of the vessel, its history, and, following the ship's disappearance, on the searches and their results.

Editor's Introduction:
Legend and Reality

The disappearance of ships and planes in the Atlantic-Caribbean area known as the Bermuda Triangle has become the subject of television and radio programs, of books and magazine articles, and of lively conversations in homes, universities, and leisure spots throughout the United States. One can hear the riddle of the Triangle discussed over luncheon counters, in stores and bowling alleys; the mysterious aspects of this contemporary legendary reality now fascinate millions.

But is not the phrase "legendary reality" a contradiction in terms? Can something be a legend and reality at the same time? Yes, and this is particularly true of events concerning the Bermuda Triangle. Around the core of reality, of actually documented losses of ships and planes, a legend has developed—that these disappearances are due to mysterious forces or entities, that vessels seem to have been "pulled down" or "lifted up" by unknown elements for puzzling and frightening reasons.

This book should help to divide reality and legend. Its contributors are authorities on the subjects they discuss. Their narratives and comments are based either on firsthand observation or on the most detailed documentation available. I am particularly grateful that Vincent H. Gaddis, the man who coined the term "Bermuda Triangle," agreed to contribute an overall survey of the subject, which represents the lead contribution to this volume, as well as a listing of Bermuda Triangle victims, which appears in the final section of the book.

The Riddle of the Bermuda Triangle has not been compiled with the intention of advancing one or another dogmatic view on the validity or cause of the phenomena of the mysterious disappearances with which it deals. Rather, by offering a forum to a variety of approaches, this book seeks to throw light on this legendary reality from several valid viewpoints.

Among the contributions to this volume is one of the last writings of Ivan T. Sanderson, the colorful, able, and energetic writer-explorer. It is to the memory of Ivan Sanderson (1911–1973), founder-director, and of Hans Stefan Santesson (1914–1975), president and chairman of the board, of the Society for the Study of the Unexplained, that this book is dedicated.

MARTIN EBON

I

MYSTERIES
OF THE
MISSING

1. Twilight Zone of Death

by Vincent H. Gaddis

The man who coined the phrase "Bermuda Triangle" now regrets that he used a term that implies specific boundaries for the inexplicable phenomena that have been recorded in the adjacent areas of the Atlantic Ocean and the Caribbean Sea. Mr. Gaddis is a veteran researcher-writer in the area of the mysterious and unknown. Among his many works is the book Mysterious Fires and Lights. *He has also contributed to this volume the most up-to-date and definitive listing of "Bermuda Triangle Victims," which forms one of the concluding sections of the book.*

IT IS a region where airplanes vanish in the sky, where ships or sometimes only the crews disappear. Draw a line from the Florida coast to Puerto Rico, then north to Bermuda and back to Florida. That's the Bermuda Triangle, a journalistic term that has joined such misnomers as "flying saucers" and the "abominable snowman." I used the name in an article in *Argosy* magazine (February 1964) and later in my book *Invisible Horizons* (Chilton, 1965).

This I now regret, since a triangle implies boundaries that contain the phenomena. Other writers have called it an oval. Richard Winer, co-producer of the television documentary *The Devil's Sea,* uses the term in the title of his book *The Devil's Triangle* (Bantam Books, 1974). But, he writes, it is not a triangle at all. "It is a trapezium, a four-sided area in which no two sides or angles are the same," he explains. "And the first four letters of the word *trapezium* more than adequately describe it." Nevertheless, the word "triangle" will continue to be used, like "saucer," and we accept it for purposes of understanding.

Actually these marine mysteries take place all around a shapeless area in the Caribbean Sea and on out into the Atlantic Ocean, including part of the Sargasso Sea, the legendary graveyard of lost ships. What distinguishes these occurrences from the usual mishaps that plague air and sea travel

3

are that they are total vanishments: no wreckage, no bodies, no oil slicks. According to reports of those who have encountered the weird forces of this oceanic twilight zone and lived to tell about it, the phenomena include startling magnetic manifestations, anomalies of vision, and radio dead zones.

After publication of my article in *Argosy*, one of the letters I received from readers was written by Gerald C. Hawkes. In 1952 my correspondent had completed a long tour of duty in Korea. With a friend, presently a surgeon in New York City, he decided to take a vacation in Bermuda. They left New York on a BOAC four-motor prop aircraft. Although there were storm clouds around, they were flying above them, and the flight was very smooth. Suddenly the huge aircraft dropped straight down a couple of hundred feet.

"The nose did not go down," Hawkes wrote, "it was as if we had suddenly stopped all forward movement and just dropped straight down. . . . We were just beginning to comprehend what had happened and were trying to get back in our seats when the plane shot straight up, forcing us down hard in our seats. It was as if a giant hand was holding the plane and jerking it up and down. The wing tips were fluctuating as much as twenty feet, and the whole plane was groaning under the strain of what seemed to be two forces, one pulling up and the other pulling down."

The up-and-down movement continued for about half an hour, gradually decreasing. After telling his frightened passengers that the aircraft would not shake itself to pieces, the captain announced that he had an even more alarming problem. He explained that he could not find Bermuda, that he was unable to make radio contact with either the United States or Bermuda. They had to reach a decision. They could turn back and land in Florida, or they could fly past Bermuda and try to establish contact with a radio ship stationed out past Bermuda. Since the strange turbulence was subsiding and they still had more than enough fuel to go back to the mainland, it was decided to continue on, try for a radioship contact, and approach Bermuda from the Atlantic side.

During the next hour the cockpit door was open and the passengers could hear the radio operator as he unsuccessfully attempted to contact the United States, Bermuda, and the radio ship. Finally, loud and clear, a voice came over the air. It was the radio ship. They got their bearings, turned back, and in a short time had Bermuda on the radio. Hawkes noticed that the sky was clear and starry, and there was no reasonable explanation for the radio blackout.

"Although this happened over ten years ago," he comments, "I am still wondering if we were a few of the lucky ones who were caught in the Bermuda Triangle, where time and space seem to disappear, but successfully made it through. I have often thought we could have been just another missing flight, down somewhere between New York and Bermuda, on the books as another mysterious disappearance."

On March 16, 1971, the Devil's Triangle and similar locations where puzzling disappearances occur were discussed on Dick Cavett's television talk show. The guests included Arthur Godfrey and the late Ivan T. Sanderson. Concerning magnetic disturbances, Godfrey said that he and other experienced fliers en route from New York to Florida usually cut across the ocean to save a hundred miles or so. When they do, they keep a wary eye on their instruments, especially the compass.

Another Devil's Sea is east of the Bonin Islands in the West Pacific south of Japan. The disappearance of fishing vessels caused the Japanese government to send a survey ship to the area. It, too, vanished. After World War II it was on the flight path between Japan and Guam, and the U.S. Air Force expressed concern over the loss of military aircraft.

It was here that Arthur Godfrey hit a radio dead zone. For an hour and a half he had no contact with the outside world, and with only four hours of gas to go. "And that's not nice!" he told his listeners. Asked by Dick Cavett if he thought such regions warranted proper scientific investigation, he replied, "Yes."

After studying locations with a high incidence of disappearances, Sanderson said there appeared to be ten such areas around the earth, precisely distributed as dipoles through the planet—five in the northern hemisphere centered some 72 degrees apart longitudinally, and five others similarly separated in the southern hemisphere but all shifted about 20 degrees to the east. Correlations of these ten anomalous areas were found only with surface ocean currents.

"However," Sanderson wrote, "both military and commercial pilots began supplying us with factual data of another nature. This was to the effect that in, or immediately around, these ten areas there appeared to be evidence of a time anomaly. By this is meant (to oversimplify) that a plane may appear to have arrived at its destination either much too soon

5

or much too late; according to its instruments on the one hand, and by ground records on the other."

If this theory is true, it would appear that the earth is a gigantic static electrical machine having not just five dipoles, represented by the ten anomalous areas or vortices, but six, the sixth pair represented by the north and south magnetic poles. A time anomaly may indicate a space warp.

And there are anomalies of vision that seem to precede some disappearances. This occurred during aviation's greatest mystery, the ill-fated Flight 19 from the former Fort Lauderdale Naval Air Station in Florida on December 5, 1945. On the afternoon of this day a squadron of five torpedo bombers was on a routine training flight out over the Atlantic. A frantic message from the flight leader came to the tower at the air station. The squadron was off course, and no land was visible. They were lost.

It was 4:00 P.M., and the sun was in the west on a clear day. The tower instructed the planes to assume bearing due west. The reply from the flight leader was startling. "We don't know which way is west," he said. "Everything is wrong ... strange. Even the ocean doesn't look as it should!" Then the five planes vanished, to be followed into oblivion by a huge Martin Mariner rescue plane that was looking for them.

And there is the tragic story of Caroline Coscio, a twenty-four-year-old Miami Beach nurse. On June 6, 1969, she rented a Cessna 172 at Pompano Beach and with a male companion began a flight to Jamaica. She refueled at Georgetown in the Bahamas, then left for Grand Turk Island, her next fueling stop. At 7:30 P.M. the tower operator on Grand Turk received a message from her stating that her direction-finding equipment was not working properly and asking for assistance.

She said she was circling "two islands, and nothing is down there." Guests at an Ambergris Cay hotel saw a plane circling overhead at that time. A jet pilot tried to help Miss Coscio with directions, but not knowing her location, he was unsuccessful. Her final message was that she was out of fuel. Searchers found no trace of the craft. The puzzle here is that the guests could see the Cessna at a time of year when the light was still quite good, yet she said "nothing is down there." If she could have seen the hotel and described it and the shape of the two cays, her location could have been determined.

Magnetic disturbances can occasionally reach a frightening peak. In December 1972, Chuck Wakely and copilot Sam

6

Mathes were flying to Miami from Bimini. Their Piper Aztec was on automatic pilot. They had just passed over Andros Island at about eight thousand feet.

"I was looking out the window," Wakely reported, "when I noticed that the wings seemed to take on a translucent effect. They were almost glowing, a bluish glow that intensified steadily. It wasn't very long before this glow flooded the cockpit, drowning out the red instrument lights. Then our instruments went crazy. The autopilot went off first. Then the rest of the electrical system became erratic. Fuel-tank gauges that had been reading three-quarters suddenly went full. Then I noticed the compass turning—not spinning, but making a steady, slow series of 360-degree revolutions. I didn't count the number of times it went around.

"We were headed straight out toward Bimini now, instead of Florida, and there was nothing we could do about it. It was late at night, and we had no horizon, no compass, and no reliable instruments; so all we could do was try to stabilize the craft by adjusting the wing flaps. Then, as we tried to contact the Nassau tower, the light started to go away and everything returned to normal. The whole thing happened in a period of five or six minutes."

I have an occasional corresponding friend, Captain Robert J. Durant, an airline pilot. We are fellow members of the Society for the Investigation of the Unexplained, established in 1965 by Ivan T. Sanderson and some associates. What may be the most shocking and close escape from the clutches of the Triangle's grim forces happened to a pilot friend of his. Naturally, the airline involved kept silent on the occurrence, and the only account of the incident is in the society's quarterly journal *Pursuit* (July 1973).

The flight was en route from San Juan to New York at a 35,000-foot altitude. The first sign of something unusual was the smooth air without even the occasional little turbulence bumps airliners experience under the best of circumstances. After the plane had flown through this unnaturally clear air for some minutes, streaks of static electricity appeared on the windshield. While this is not unusual, it is almost always experienced while flying through heavy clouds, and most especially through the tops of thunderstorm clouds. These tiny streamers of purplish electrical discharges are harmless.

As time passed, the static discharges became so strong that they covered the entire windshield with a bright white glow. Captain Durant, with all his experience, had never seen or heard of this phenomenon. The jet was still passing through

7

turbulence-free air. The weird electrical glow increased its intensity.

At this time the aircraft was on autopilot, which was set to hold the course straight and level. Suddenly the copilot noticed that the autopilot monitor on his side of the cockpit indicated the plane had left its straight course and was turning. Checking, the captain glanced at his gyro horizon to confirm the turn, but there was no bank-angle indication. There was a discrepancy between the captain's and the copilot's instruments on each side of the cockpit. Both the gyros and the compasses were giving conflicting readouts.

Captain Durant's account continues: "This is a very serious situation indeed to a big jet. They are flown almost entirely by reference to the instruments. Instrument failures occur, and there are standard procedures for remedying such failures; this instrument failure was definitely 'not in the books.' There was no means of determining which instrument—if any—was functioning properly. The crew was now in an emergency situation."

As insurance against a total loss of electrical power, there was a small, battery-operated gyro horizon on board. The captain used it to see which of the other two gyros was indicating correctly, and discovered, to his bewilderment, that it was giving an entirely different readout than the two installed in the cockpit.

They were now about one hundred miles south of Bermuda, and the island has an excellent long-range radar system. The captain decided to fly entirely on the battery-operated gyro, and he requested the tower at Bermuda to provide him radar assistance with the navigation and emergency landing clearance. They arrived without further incident.

Airport mechanics could find no cause for the malfunctioning instruments. Captain Durant's friend had never heard of the Triangle until that fateful night. Then he did! A mechanic poked his head into the cockpit and said, "You know what's wrong? You've just flown through the Bermuda Triangle!"

The airline's technical center in New York was contacted by telephone. The engineers there insisted that what had happened was an impossibility. After several days of looking and shaking their puzzled heads, the island mechanics gave up. The jet was flown back to New York in daylight without incident.

Then the engineering experts went to work. They decided that the electrical system and all of the instruments showed signs of having been subjected "to an extremely strong electrical shock, probably the result of being struck by a lightning bolt." Both the wiring and the instruments were completely replaced. But there had been no lightning bolt. Pilots know when lightning strikes a plane. There is a bright flash and a sharp report, not a sustained static glow.

It was later learned that another airliner, a four-engine turboprop from Great Britain, had landed at Bermuda reporting trouble with all instruments. Unfortunately, Captain Durant's friend was so concerned about his own problem that he failed to talk to the British crew.

Intensive magnetic-electrical phenomena. Anomalies of vision. Time warps. Radio dead zones. Have these missing planes and vessels passed through what Sanderson calls "vile vortices," occasional openings into other realms, dimensions, worlds? Perhaps they simply and totally disintegrate into a cloud of atoms under the pressure of a titanic force. Fantastic occurrences suggest fantastic theories. Are the crews of seaworthy abandoned ships kidnapped by UFO's? In several instances the crews were missing, but dogs, the ships' mascots, were still aboard. It is a superstition of the sea that your doom is sealed if a mascot is left behind.

Does the answer lie beneath the sea? Apollo astronauts on the way to the moon marveled at the white water in the Triangle area, and high-flying pilots have also commented on it. It is as though there were continual agitation stirring well below the surface. Is there a sophisticated power source that may have been left on the ocean floor when a civilization superior to ours sank beneath the waves? Does it occasionally create magnetic fields that doom ships and aircraft?

Mammoth manmade stone ruins have been discovered in about thirty feet of water west of Bimini. Edgar Cayce, the famed sleeping prophet, placed Atlantis in this general area, adding that the lost continent's inhabitants derived tremendous energy from crystals. These power sources seem to have been similar to masers and lasers.

Another theory is that there is a parallel three-dimensional world interpenetrating our own world, coexisting and occupying the same space. Between these worlds there are occasionally openings. Objects and beings from our world could pass through these openings or vortices into this parallel world. There is a growing belief that this may be where the UFO's originate.

Dead men—men who have permanently vanished—tell no tales. If we are to solve the Triangle mystery, we must study the accounts of those who have encountered the forces there

9

and survived. It has been suggested that we are not advanced enough to solve the UFO enigma, that we will have to wait for the new knowledge and discoveries of the twenty-first century or beyond. This may also be true of the Triangle riddle.

And despite our technology, despite the swift wings that have diminished travel time, despite the instantaneous voices of radio heard afar, a mile is still a mile and the dangers of the sea still exist. There is still a vast unknown, a misty limbo of the lost feared by our forefathers.

2. Jinxed Seas

by C. Winn Upchurch

The pattern observed in the Bermuda Triangle has been noted elsewhere, and this account deals specifically with the menace to shipping around Sable Island, off Nova Scotia, Canada, in the North Atlantic. The author, a veteran observer of naval activities and risks, views the Sable Island menace against the background of the whole pattern of mysterious and inexplicable disappearances. This article, written originally for the U.S. Coast Guard Alumni Association Bulletin, *may be regarded as a particularly detached and comprehensive summary of the subject.*

PROBABLY no other areas of the world's waterways have taken a greater toll of men and ships than a floating island and a "devil sea," both located off the Atlantic Coast.

Thousands of vessels and tens of thousands of lives have been lost at Sable Island, off Nova Scotia, and in a rectangular area of the Atlantic extending a few hundred miles from the coast and bounded on the north by Bermuda and on the south by Cuba.

There is a reason for Sable's menace to navigation, but no logical explanation why so many men and ships have been lost in the Devil Sea, most of them vanishing without a trace—no wreckage, no bodies, no clues.

Not even planes have been spared by the jinxed sea.

While flying over this body of water planes have vanished

without a trace, leaving no radioed distress calls or wreckage that might give a clue to the mysteries.

Sable Island—a moving spit of sand southeast of Nova Scotia—is known as "The Graveyard of the Atlantic."

Since its discovery more than 450 years ago, this treacherous isle has trapped and destroyed more than five hundred vessels and ten thousand lives. The island, which moves eastward about one-eighth of a mile a year, is littered with wreckage of ships.

It is believed that two million dollars in gold is hidden in ships' strongboxes scattered in the sand and surf. Authority for this is in the *Disaster Books* in the Marine Library of the Atlantic Mutual Insurance Company.

Before the establishment of two lights, a radio beacon, and a lifesaving station Sable was a deadly menace to navigation. It is hardly distinguishable from the ocean on an overcast day and it is surrounded by vicious eddies.

"Where one day there is open sea," notes Atlantic Mutual's *Disaster Books* of the shifting, elusive island, "the next will find sandy shoals upon which any boat drawing more than a few feet of water will come to grief."

The history of Sable opens with a shipwreck.

In the early 1500's the *Admiral*, sailing from England to establish a colony in Newfoundland, foundered with one hundred men. In 1801 the British transport *Amelia* was lost with all but one of two hundred aboard. A schooner searching for survivors also sank, and again there was but a single survivor.

The most tragic Sable Island disaster was in 1898, when five hundred lives were lost in the collision of the *La Bourgogne* and *Cromartyshire*.

The most unusual shipwreck was that of the *Myrtle*. Wrecked and abandoned in January 1840, she freed herself and drifted to the Azores in July. She was repaired and sailed again.

In the days before the light and lifesaving stations, Sable Island was populated only by two seventeenth-century ghosts and a herd of wild ponies. One of the ghosts, according to recorded lore at Atlantic Mutual, is a French nobleman banished by the king. The other is an Englishman who goes about singing psalm tunes, so the legend goes.

The ponies are the descendants of a herd of shipwrecked horses.

Sable was truly a sinister island.

Some sixty ships and planes have sailed or flown into the

11

"jinxed-waters" void off the Atlantic Coast and have been swallowed up.

In March 1866 the Swedish barg *Lotta,* out of Goteborg, bound for Havana, vanished off the north coast of Haiti. Two years later, the Spanish merchantman *Viego* similarly disappeared in the same locale.

The British training frigate *Atlanta* left Bermuda in January 1880 for England and was never heard from again. She carried a crew of 250 cadets and sailors.

Four years later the Italian schooner *Miramon* bound for New Orleans vanished in this patch of ocean.

In the above cases searchers were puzzled by a complete absence of flotsam. No clues as to the fate of the vessels were ever found.

The first victim of this "devil sea" to receive world-wide publicity was the U.S. Naval collier *Cyclops,* displacing 19,500 tons, considered the last word in marine construction when she was built in 1910.

On March 4, 1918, she sailed from Barbados for Norfolk, Virginia. She carried a crew of 221 men and 57 passengers. She was due in Norfolk on March 13. She never arrived.

One of the most intensive sea searches ever undertaken failed to locate a single clue as to the *Cyclops* disappearance.

The possibility of a German submarine attack was studied, but produced no proof. The *Cyclops* carried full wireless equipment and lifeboats. After the war, records of the German Imperial Admiralty showed there were no U-boats anywhere near the area between the time the *Cyclops* sailed and the period of her disappearance.

In more recent years victims of the Devil Sea have been: American freighter *Cotopaxi,* lost in January 1925 when en route from Charleston, South Carolina, to Havana; cargo tramp *Sudoffco,* out of Port Newark and bound for Puerto Rico, vanished completely; October 1931 the Norwegian *Stavanger* disappeared south of Cat Islands in the Bahamas; the U.S. freighter *Sandra* in 1950 sailed from Savannah, Georgia, last seen off St. Augustine, Florida.

The only similarity among the disappearance of the above vessels was that all carried radios, and none sounded distress calls. None of the ships encountered rough weather. Despite wide-spread searches not a single clue was ever found.

There was a more recent vanishing act that did leave a trace—a solitary floating life jacket.

The *Marine Sulphur Queen,* a modern tanker, left Beaumont, Texas, on the morning of February 2, 1963, bound for

Norfolk. A day later her final radio message was recorded, placing the vessel near Key West in the Straits of Florida. Then, a curtain of silence.

A wide-spread search by the Coast Guard, using planes and cutters, produced only the lone life jacket, found on a calm sea about forty miles southwest of the tanker's last known position.

Nothing else was ever found. No drifting lifeboats, no oil slicks, not a clue to the fate of the thirty-nine men who had sailed from Beaumont on the *Sulphur Queen*.

The absence of bodies has been the most baffling aspect of these disappearances. In most shipwrecks, sharks and barracudas rip into floating corpses, some parts of which wash up on shores.

But not so in the strange disappearances of ships in these jinxed waters.

However, the most perplexing disappearance in this void involved not ships, but planes.

Five Avenger torpedo bombers roared down the runways of the U.S. Naval Air Station at Fort Lauderdale, Florida, on the afternoon of Wednesday, December 5, 1945, swung out over the Atlantic, and were never heard from again.

To further complicate the mystery a large Martin Mariner flying boat with a crew of thirteen took off from Fort Lauderdale to join the search and it too disappeared.

The five bomber planes carried a total of fourteen men.

Ten minutes after the flying boat departed the control tower lost radio contact with it and never established it again. As night approached it became obvious to the men at the base they had lost the rescuer as well as the five planes it was sent out to rescue.

A dozen aircraft scouted the area before the sun went down. The sea was calm, winds average, skies clear, but not a single clue was ever found.

Later the search was greatly expanded, including the aircraft carrier *Solomons* and twenty-one additional vessels. Some 260 U.S. planes scoured the ocean from above, aided by 30 Royal Air Force planes from British bases in the Bahamas. Even land parties systematically worked up and down the Florida coast looking for clues.

The search even extended into the Gulf of Mexico although the missing planes had flown eastward, into the Atlantic. Hundreds of volunteers covered almost a quarter of a million square miles in one of the greatest searches ever conducted, but not a single clue was ever found to solve the baffling mystery.

Ultimately the authorities admitted: "We were not able to even make a good guess as to what happened."

Today the fate of the missing planes remains as complex and strange as it was on that day in 1945 when twenty-seven flyers went out over the Atlantic and were never heard from again.

Indeed, men who go down to the sea in ships are paying a bitter price.

Despite modern navigational aids, the number of shipwrecks is going up, not only in the two spots mentioned here but all over the world.

Despite radio communications, ships still disappear on the high seas as mysteriously as did the crew of the *Marie Celeste*, the ghost vessel found in the Mediterranean with sails set and not a soul aboard in 1872.

In 1967, 337 ships, totaling 832,803 tons of the world's merchant fleet, foundered, collided, caught fire, ran aground, or were otherwise lost. These figures from Lloyd's Register of Shipping in London were the worst recorded in peacetime.

Fifteen of these ships simply vanished—not just small ones like the 650-ton West German trawler *Johannes Kruff*, last reported in the North Atlantic fishing grounds near Greenland, but large freighters like the 8,338-ton *Sante Fe* of Chile, traveling down the Pacific coast with a cargo of iron ore.

It is a deep mystery as to what happened to the *Sante Fe* but it is believed she sank in bad weather. Altogether more than thirteen hundred ships have died this century. Among the worst tragedies was the 10,000-ton liner *Waratah*, which disappeared off the South African coast in 1909 with four hundred passengers and crew, never to be seen again.

Shipping experts say it is hard to pin a general cause of the increasing number of casualties, but nearly half are due to stranding on rocks, sand banks or sunken wrecks.

They feel the figures show some countries, including those operating flags of convenience, should raise their standards of maintenance, crew training and navigation.

Nations with the biggest fleets, Japan, Britain and the United States, have a low rate of loss. The countries with much smaller fleets, Lebanon, Hong Kong, Panama, Greece, Italy, Liberia and Brazil, lost the most ships last year.

One British shipping expert said: "If we regard our own

14

standards as among the best, clearly others are second best or third best.

"Generally one can say that two elements are involved: personnel—that is the masters and officers—and equipment.

"One could probably take the general view that equipment is not always up to standard. But if personnel have indifferent equipment, then they know its limitations and take account of it.

"Basically there is never any excuse for going aground if the ship has power and can impel itself.

"Navigation is essentially, like democracy, a matter for eternal vigilance. It's a hard rule to follow but one must always be intensely careful."

The Inter-Governmental Maritime Consultative Organization (IMCO) is looking into questions of equipment, crew training and supervision in an attempt to cut down on the alarming rise of lost ships and men.

However, it would appear that nothing man can do can prevent the strange disappearances in the jinxed waters off the Atlantic coast, where so many men and ships have vanished.

3. Worldwide Seas of Mystery

by Ivan T. Sanderson

Ivan T. Sanderson, who died on February 20, 1973, was a pioneer in the study of the unexplained, but also an explorer and writer on a number of very concrete and lively subjects. His father established the first game reserve in Kenya, East Africa, and Ivan Sanderson spent much of his life traveling in exotic parts of the world, often collecting animals for zoos and specimens for such institutions as the Chicago Natural History Museum. He was also active in radio and television, conducting round-table and interview programs. At one time he had a summer roadside zoo in New Jersey, and a winter traveling animal exhibit. He organized the Society for the Investigation of the Unexplained in 1965. Among his books are The Continents We Live On, Uninvited Visitors, *and* Invisible Residents.

LLOYD'S of London has kept tabs on world shipping since the formal initiation of insurance as a business a few hundred years ago. Today, shipping insurance is a worldwide enterprise, and ship losses are analyzed and regularly reported under six headings: 1) foundered, swamped, or burst asunder due to the sea alone; 2) burned; 3) collided; 4) wrecked, on rocks, shores, or underwater hazards; 5) missing; and, 6) other causes. "Missing" means disappearing, without trace (wreckage, bodies, etc.) and without any distress calls or signals being picked up.

From the first of January 1961 to the end of 1970, Lloyd's listed 2,766 shipping losses: 1,136 by wrecking; 771 by foundering; and 70 under disappearing. The largest of the last lot was a 10,000-tonner named the *Milton Iatridis* out of New Orleans, Louisiana, with a cargo of vegetable oils and caustic soda, bound for Cape Town, South Africa. Next in size was the *Ithaca Island,* a 7,426-ton vessel with a load of grain out of Norfolk, Virginia, bound for Manchester, England. Their disappearances occurred somewhere near Bermuda. Take a look at a map and see if that rings a bell. Does the name "Bermuda Triangle" sound familiar? If not, then you should know that this area in the Atlantic is notorious for the disappearances of many ships and planes under very mysterious circumstances.

Ships have been foundering and "disappearing" at sea since time immemorial, an accepted fact until comparatively recent times when ship-to-shore contact by radio was established. Then it began being noticed that one of the six categories of lost ships—those that "disappeared"—constituted an unusual class. Then came airplanes. Though usually smaller, planes are much more closely in touch with land bases, as well as in communication with each other, with ships, and, in the case of military craft, with submarines. What's more, aircraft can be "watched" visually and by radar to the horizon, and then by radio contact beyond. Thus, when they started disappearing the whole business became a lot more "sticky."

Even if a plane is out of radio and radar contact, its general course is plotted and logged—unless it's a private plane—and if it "founders" (disintegrates in the air due to atmospheric conditions) or is "wrecked" (crashes, burns, or collides), it invariably leaves something on the surface of the sea (or land), even if it's only an oil slick. Yet, the moment transoceanic flight became common, during and after World War II, planes also began to disappear (while they were in contact, for example), as opposed to just being "unaccounted for." But war is war, and nobody had the time to investigate. After the war things took on quite another aspect when the following incident occurred:

On December 5, 1945, five TBM Avenger torpedo bombers left the Fort Lauderdale Naval Air Station in Florida on a routine patrol. They were scheduled to fly some 160 miles due east out over the Atlantic, then travel north for 40 miles, and then return directly to base. The planes took off at 2:00 P.M. and were first heard from at 3:35 P.M., at which time it became clear that all was not well. They had no idea where they were, said they didn't know even which way was west, and that "Everything is wrong ... strange. We can't be sure of any direction. Even the ocean doesn't look as it should." The base listened to exchanges between the five pilots for about another hour, and at 4:25 the flight leader reported to Fort Lauderdale, "We don't know where we are. We think we must be about 225 miles northeast of base ... it looks like we are." And that was the last ever heard or seen of the five TBMs. Within minutes a Martin Mariner flying boat was airborne to search for the planes; and within fifteen minutes, it, too, vanished. The resultant search operation was probably the most extensive in history up to that time and covered thousands of square miles, but no trace of either the five TBMs or the Martin Mariner was ever found.

If you'll take another look at the map, you will see that this incident was grossly misnamed. After a lot of research, I have come to the conclusion that the basis for this was purely semantic: The first newsman to report the incident stated correctly that the flight was on a *triangular* course. Only later did others note that the apex of this triangle was in line with Bermuda. Then in 1964 that splendid reporter, Vincent Gaddis, entitled his story "The Bermuda Triangle," and for one of those inexplicable reasons it had a "ring to it" that caught the public's fancy. The name confuses the public, but it did lead to a "story." And what a story!

Vincent Gaddis followed up the story lead and did the initial reportorial research, and it was he who prompted me to plunge into the act. That was also the year (1966) in which a group of us founded the Society for the Investigation of the Unexplained; and when it came to drawing up our research and development prospectives, the Triangle was unanimously voted fourth on the list for immediate investigation, though it was a highly esoteric item then, compared to what it has become today, only seven years later.

It was then listed simply as "The Bermuda Triangle" and

took fourth place after: 1) "Abominable Snowman," another semantic abomination, meaning as yet uncaught and unidentified, ultraprimitive human beings or hominids: 2) "Marine and Freshwater Monsters," as yet uncaught or unidentified animals of large size reported in lakes, some rivers, and seas; and, 3) UFOs, or unidentified aerial (or aquatic) *objects* as opposed to UAPs or unidentified atmospheric (or aerial) phenomena. It's also interesting to note that the fifth was "I.T.F."—instant transference of solids through solids; and, 6) "T.T.T." or transference of solids through time. The significance, as opposed to any mere coincidence, of this will become apparent later.

When we assembled our material on the Bermuda Triangle, we encountered several startling surprises. The first came from our old friend, and now one of our members, Vince Gaddis, who urged us to start digging further into the famous "Devil's Sea" in the western Pacific, lying between Japan and the Bonin Islands, which he had first brought to the public's attention in an article.

This area has been known for centuries by the Japanese but, thank God, it never got tabbed as a "triangle." When countless ships disappeared there, and then both Japanese and U.S. military planes plotted the area during World War II, its shape turned out to be a sort of "blob" or oval that is pitched at an angle of about 25 degrees SW to NE. By this time, moreover, the records we found of disappearances in the Bermuda Triangle had begun to point up a very similar, if not identical, conformation, of just about the same size and also "pitched" at about the same angle.

My education has been solidly grounded on a geographical basis, and I always reach for an atlas or globe the moment any research project crops up, regardless of the location or size of the area concerned. And it was this "map grabbing" that really set us off on the long path that has led to the discoveries I shall now describe.

The first thing that struck us was that both these areas—which we found to be better defined as lozenges, for the sake of more graphic precision—lay athwart the same latitudes. Their "centers," which could only be rather arbitrarily defined, were both at 36 degrees N. Then one of those coincidences that seem so noncoincidental occurred. Two submarines, one French and one Israeli, disappeared in the Mediterranean, and four small vessels just vanished in fine weather between the coast of Portugal, Morocco, and the island of Madeira.

18

Immediately our investigative-research society was snowed under with an avalanche of press clippings and letters from our members both here and abroad and from people we had never heard of (in half a dozen languages). Their question was: "Do you think that the western Mediterranean is the center of another of your 'lozenges'?" After taking another look at the globe, I called a meeting of all the members I could round up with training in geodesy. They flew in from all over the country. But it was an engineer—Alfred D. Bielek—who arrived at the first concrete suggestion.

We started our conference with a Mercator Projection of a World Map, and Bielek pointed out that this newly inspected area also lay athwart the 36th Parallel of North latitude and (from the reports we had on the new area and in a whole file of more historical data) it also formed a lozenge of the same shape and size that tilted SW to NE with its center somewhere near the borders of Morocco and Algeria on the southern Mediterranean shore.

Then, still another purely coincidental item arrived in the next day's mail. This was a letter from a woman we had never heard of, and who obviously knew nothing of our work and seemed not to have heard of the Bermuda Triangle. For many years, she had been worried about something which had come to her attention during World War II when she was employed by American Intelligence in what is now Pakistan. She reported that large planes were flying between what was then India and Russia as an adjunct to military aid supplied by the Allies via Iran, etc. Some of these planes were used for transporting gold bullion, and to the considerable distress of the Allies, a number of planes disappeared over Afghanistan. What had intrigued this woman was that in at least two cases the gold was allegedly found by hill tribesmen but *no part of any airplane was ever found!*

Once again, we reached for our globes and slide rules. Why? Because this gave us a *fourth* area of "disappearances" (and most bizarre disappearances at that) *over land*. What's more, it suggested something else; for when we measured the longitudinal distance from the western Mediterranean lozenge to Afghanistan to the Bonin Sea, it came out at exactly 72-degree intervals. Further, from the western Mediterranean to the Bermuda Triangle was also exactly 72 degrees.

Now 72 degrees is exactly one-fifth of a circle (360 degrees). With four lozenges in a line from the western Atlantic to the western Pacific, could there be a fifth; and where would it fall? It turned out that it *should* be to the northeast of the Hawaiian Islands in the northern Pacific.

I'll never forget the silence after that. Five of us, with either extensive or partial scientific or technological training and knowledge, and four others in the news media, were all just sitting there staring at geographer Bielek! But it was an electromagnetic engineer who broke the deadlock. "Look," he said, "nature is seldom exact, but it is physically precise. What do you know of affairs in that northeastern Pacific area?" Our executive secretary and librarian, Marion Fawcett, a sort of animated computer, readily admitted that we had absolutely nothing on it. (Little did we know then what was to come later.)

While all the above was happening, a little mental "worm" began wiggling away at the back of my mind. During the months we had been wrestling with the Bermuda and the Bonin data and collecting more, I had been quietly digging into a project of my own. The Southern Hemisphere.

I found, through correspondence and a lot of research, that there were three most alarming areas of "disappearances" there also: 1) off the southeast coast of Argentina; 2) off the southeast coast of South Africa; and, 3) off the southeast coast of Australia, namely the Tasman Sea. Once again, I grabbed the globes and reversed them on their stands so that the South Pole was at the top. Then, I lightly traced the outlines of these three areas (or lozenges) and asked the slide-rule boys to go to work. What did they find? Two of the areas were exactly 72 degrees apart and both on 36 degrees *south* latitude, while the third was 144 degrees from the nearest on either side (144 is twice 72). And where did the "missing" two fall? One in the east Indian Ocean; the other smack in the middle of the great oceanic area of the southeast Pacific.

This was as far as we got at that meeting, but then still another "coincidence," or whatever you may choose to call it, landed on my desk; again totally unsolicited and from somebody whom we had never heard from or of. It was from a young woman in the Southwest who stated she had two brothers, one in the Navy and the other in the Air Force, and that they had told her stories they had heard from others in the services. Because of the nature of the stories, she had shown them an article of mine on "Vile Vortices." Their immediate reaction was there were two more "vortices," one in the North Pacific and *one in the South Pacific!*

This was startling enough but within a month an old friend

20

of mine who had never heard of any of the above, but whose life has been devoted to the *history* of exploration, particularly by whalers and sealers, wrote me extensively on the matter of Kerguelen and other isolated islands of the subantarctic Indian Ocean; and he just happened to mention an area of "deadliness" in the empty western part off the southwestern coast of Australia. On further inquiry, this proved to be right athwart 36 degrees S and at 72 degrees *east* of the South African blob, and *west* of the Tasman Sea one.

There was just too much "coincidence" in all this, especially for the mathematicians, geographers, geodesists, and electromagnetic engineers. Another special meeting was called at the request of the last group.

In the meantime, a geophysicist had tried a little experiment. Our globes were hollow metal spheres, and he asked permission to drive skewers through them from each of the five "points" in the Northern Hemisphere to the center of the Earth and see where they came out in the Southern Hemisphere. They all protruded on the 36-degree south latitude, *but* all just 23.5 degrees away from the five southern lozenges! He admitted he had thought the five pairs might be exactly opposite and thus dipoles of an electromagnetic nature. This 23.5-degree shift completely confounded him and his technical brethren. But somebody pointed out that 23.5 degrees is the angle at which the Earth's axis leans as it goes around the Sun. Could this mean anything?

While all this was going on, we had been consulting every expert we could find in the hope of correlating these, by this time, ten areas, which we now called "anomalies," with any other kinds of anomalies, such as gravitic, magnetic, heavy mineral concentration, seismographic activity, and so forth; but none correlated—*except one*.

This was the somewhat startling discovery that all the "lozenges" over water—all but the one over Afghanistan, and the one partly over Northwest Africa—exactly coincided with the great oceanic "maelstroms" that exist where cold currents meet warm ones, setting up giant whirligigs. Later, meteorologists pointed out that they are also "areas of semipermanent high pressure." What could this mean?

No scientist had anything to offer, but they did stick their professional necks way out, and in a manner that I never encountered before. It took a physicist, Dr. John Carstiou, whose specialty is gravity (and who first promulgated in mathematical formulas the theoretical and quite probable existence of a *second* gravitational force), to make a concrete

21

suggestion. He stated that such a force (although classed as "weak") would most likely manifest itself in the form of vortices arranged on a regular geometric basis on the surface of an individual solid mass such as Earth. Moreover, since such vortices as we know of turn clockwise in the Northern Hemisphere and counterclockwise in the Southern, there would seem to be every reason to suppose that other forces, such as this so-called Gravity II, would conform.

Having been more or less forced into acceptance of the fact that there appear to be ten equally spaced areas on the surface of Earth where "funny things happen"—like the disappearance of planes and ships or the *early* arrival of planes that would require 500-mile-an-hour winds to make the planes so many hours early, even though there weren't any such winds—the author published what the society had learned. Still another peculiar thing then happened.

I was invited by a friend in the television field—Dick Cavett—to appear on his talk show and debate this whole business with a still older friend, Arthur Godfrey. Arthur and I have known each other since early television days, post-World War II. He has been a flier for much of his life, and in two previous appearances on Dick's show the Bermuda Triangle question arose; Arthur made mincemeat of it. Thus, Dick was courteous enough to ask me in advance if I minded being put through the meat grinder. I assured him that I didn't, the show being the thing, and that I felt quite competent to argue for my side of the story.

Well, we went on the air, and Arthur floored both of us, the audience, and the studio crew, by grabbing the globe on which I had marked all the "lozenges" and telling the most incredible *firsthand* facts about them. Arthur Godfrey is not a man to be treated lightly, and his integrity is beyond reproach. But there he sat (a man who had already expressed himself on the air as regarding the whole lozenge-triangle controversy as a lot of bunk) with my globe in his hands, telling several million people what he had *experienced*. And he gave it three strong enunciations.

First, he told what happened when he was flying around the world in a two-engine jet (his flight was widely reported by the mass media). While flying over the "Devil's Sea," his compasses, other instruments, and radio had gone off for nearly an hour. He added that: "When you've got only about four hours of gas, that's not nice."

Next, he moved the globe around so the camera could focus on the area between Hawaii and the northwest coast of our mainland. He told that he was to have flown back to the mainland on the big experimental plane called the *Mars*, but that his incoming flight was late and he missed the "boat," as it were, the *Mars* taking off without him. But he watched her on radar, when . . . suddenly, *"phooph!"* . . . and Arthur snapped his fingers at the camera—*"She just wasn't there anymore!"*

I was so stunned that I just sat there speechless, but Dick jumped in with a question. In reply, Arthur repeated very simply that this great plane was there one second and gone the next. And, he added, ". . . they never found *anything;* not even a tiny oil slick." You could hear the audience suck in its collective breath. But that wasn't all.

After a station break and a commercial, Arthur again grabbed my globe and, turning directly to the camera, showed the Bermuda lozenge. Turning it so that north was straight up, he pointed out how our East Coast really runs from southwest to northeast, and then said that fliers (in private planes) go back and forth all the time from New York to Florida. If they cut straight across that area, he said, they can save one hundred miles or so, but they just skirt around a bit to the west to keep out of it! And this came from none other than Arthur Godfrey, on the air, on one of the biggest national TV shows! If I hadn't heard a tape of the audio, I simply would not have believed it myself. But two more things happened.

We got a letter from a woman who regularly travels to the West Indies and described herself as a member of the "jet set." She wanted to know if it was "safe" to fly to the West Indies, stating that friends had recently been terribly upset when informed that their flight from Puerto Rico to Florida would take 2½ *hours;* the reason airline officials reportedly gave them was *they had to fly around the Bermuda Triangle.*

There has been an awful lot of nonsense spoken about and published on the theme that both military and commercial airlines have been told not to fly over this area. We have delved into this, and all I can say is we have *never* received *one iota* of evidence that any such instructions have *ever* been given to either by *anybody.* One member of our society who is a commercial airline pilot termed this woman's report absolute rubbish; in fact, he regularly flies that route himself. (He suggested that possibly a flight had been rerouted to avoid a storm and that someone with a "sense of humor" gave them the Bermuda Triangle explanation. On the other hand, he admits he keeps an awfully keen eye on his instruments while flying through the area!)

The fact is literally millions of people sail and fly through this area every year without any trouble ... except for some extremely odd and unnerving reports by people who ought to know what they're talking about. These reports prompted us to follow up the letter, and we uncovered a whole new aspect of the matter. The reports were from professional fliers, and when they got into the act, they brought to light absolutely concrete evidence—backed by copies of official flight records, and so forth—that there are *time* anomalies and that a very high percentage of them appear to center upon our ten "lozenges."

Second, they pointed out another fact that all of us had missed—there aren't ten but *twelve* such areas; the other two are the North and South Poles! Of course, we don't have any records of ships or subs "disappearing" from either of these; and quite naturally in the case of the Antarctic, as it is a continent. The record of "missing" planes over the North Pole is meager, and the few cases there are seem to be accounted for by normal explanations. The oddity of the North Pole (at least) is that several space and time anomalies have been alleged, both by fliers and those crossing the ice on sled or foot.

If the Poles are accepted as the sixth pair of odd spots on our globe, they complete an equitriangulation of the surface of our Earth. We still know darned little about the South Pole, but we know a very great deal now about the North Pole. And it was the pilots who suggested that we start trying to correlate the gravitic, magnetic, and other peculiarities of the polar regions. Once again, we couldn't correlate any known anomalies of this nature or any oddities special to either the north polar ocean and ice raft or the south polar ice-cap with this mystery, *except* once again the district suggestion of something being wrong with "time" in the areas. A few fliers and travelers over the north polar ice raft have hinted at such; but then, compasses don't work normally there; often for weeks on end you can't get a fix on a star, and the ice raft itself moves both circularly as a whole and reciprocally among its ice floes, bergs, and so on. Even with the most modern and sophisticated instruments, it is often almost impossible to find out just where you are, where you're headed, and how far you're going. No wonder some explorers and other travelers believed that they had gone too far too fast or vice versa.

The result of all this is that we now have concrete evidence that there are "time anomalies" (early arrival of planes, etc.); that those definitely recorded occur with a high degree of frequency in some of the twelve lozenges; that there are rumors, hints, and statements that they occur in the rest. As a result, if these blobs are situated where they are alleged to be, they form a very precise (trigonometrical) grid covering our Earth like a vast fish net of triangles with equilateral sides, thus there ought to be—or must be—some logical explanation. Since no other known physical cause fits the case, we can but fall back on the only one that has proved out so far. That is, something goes wrong with *time* in these areas.

If Lloyd's of London differentiates between "disappearances" and all other known, tried, and true disappearances, we should, I feel, contemplate the matter very seriously. And when both commercial and military flight logs demonstrate one possibility for "popping in and popping out" of our Universe, as it were, I really do think that it's about time we took this matter seriously. I wish only that I could get an overall, worldwide, detailed list of "disappearing" planes. But we are working on it.

4. Avenging the Avengers

by Edward E. Costain

Interpretation of the Bermuda Triangle phenomena has ranged widely, in terms of both material and theoretical explanations. Edward E. Costain adds a new dimension to this lively debate. Mr. Costain, who received his B.A. from Fordham University and his M.A. from New York University, served with the Office of Naval Information (1943–1946), later worked as a free-lance journalist, and returned to government service during the Korean War. He is at present active as a writer and lecturer.

LATE on wintry Saturday nights, when the occult buffs gather around beer-stained backroom tables, it's an odds-on bet somebody will bring up the hoary tale of how five Navy planes once vanished in midair in an eerie and frightening mystery. Then there are dark murmurings of holes in the sky, of warps in space-time, and of temporal or physical displacements to another century or another cosmos. The farther-out speculations of such quantum physicists as Max Planck and Werner Heisenberg get more free plugs in a few minutes than their authors could have hoped for in a lifetime. And much is made of a Navy spokesman's statement that the planes disappeared as completely as if they had flown off to Mars.

The five planes concerned are those torpedo bombers that took off from the Fort Lauderdale, Florida, Naval Air Station on the afternoon of December 5, 1945. They were in contact with the base control tower up to the moment they vanished. A Naval Board of Inquiry said that it was "unable even to make a good guess as to what had happened." Just to put the capper to a great occult tale, the huge Martin flying boat that went to look for the bombers disappeared, too.

The story is such a classic that it seems a shame to disturb it. Yet that is just what I intend to do. And here's why.

We live in a world filled with more strange events, aberrant reactions, and paranormal phenomena than our Elizabethan-age science can cope with. By studying the events that are truly strange, we enlarge our knowledge of the cosmos in which we live. But we frequently find that our way is cluttered by a lot of events that are only apparently strange, merely speciously paranormal. Such events, and the hairbrained hypotheses erected upon them, serve as stumbling blocks in the serious investigator's path.

Recently we have been deluged by volume after volume of unexplained facts, shaped this time around as evidence for prehistoric visitations of this planet by godlike charioteers from outer space. The same bulk of evidence was used by Donnelley to support his Atlantis theories a century ago. And fifty years ago, Churchward used it to make much of Mu.

In some weird intellectual regression to a darker age, we find that classic classroom examples of multiple personality have been recast as evidence for demonic possession.

Such hypotheses are usually erected with scant regard for whether or not the events used as their foundations are truly paranormal or not. Very often the events are made to seem paranormal by limiting the possibilities of what might actually have happened. If gratuitous restrictions are imposed upon a set of circumstances, anything arising from that set can be given a paranormal cast. Usually such restrictions arise from a lack of knowledge, experience, or insight on the part of the investigator. This may give you an idea of what I mean.

In a popular saloon puzzle, you are required to draw four straight lines through an array of nine dots, passing through each dot only once, and not lifting your pencil from the paper. Here are the dots.

And here is how it is done.

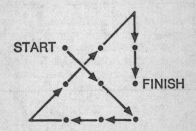

Aha! you say. *But you went outside the square!*

What square? We're not dealing with a square; we're dealing with nine dots. It was you who imposed upon yourself the restriction of a square and thus introduced a factor that made it impossible for you to solve the problem.

If an investigator persists in seeing dots as squares, he can make a mystery out of just about anything he chooses. For instance, the square researcher, hearing that UFO's make flight changes at g-stresses that would crush any living tissue we know, concludes that they must be piloted by Super Beings. Were he only to look at the dots, he would say, "Well, they are quite apparently not piloted by anyone, then, and are nothing more mysterious than somebody else's unmanned space probes."

With that sort of thinking in mind, let's see if we can

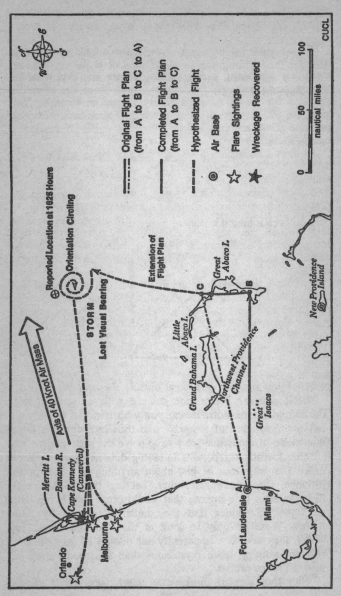

N
W E
S

Orlando

Merritt I.
Banana R.
Cape Kennedy
(Canaveral)

Melbourne

Miami

Fort Lauderdale A

Axis of 40 Knot Air Mass

STORM

Lost Visual Bearing

Reported Location at 1625 Hours

Orientation Circling

Extension of Flight Plan

Great Abaco I.

Great Abaco I.

C

B

New Providence Island

Little Abaco I.

Grand Bahama I.

Northwest Providence Channel

Great Isaacs

Original Flight Plan (from A to B to C to A)

Completed Flight Plan (from A to B to C)

Hypothesized Flight

Air Base

Flare Sightings

Wreckage Recovered

0   50   100
nautical miles

CUCL

28

break some of the squares in the case of the missing torpedo bombers down into manageable dots.

Let me recapitulate the story as it stands on available records. However, during World War II and in the period immediately afterward, accident records were not kept with the thoroughness with which they have been since the establishment of the Naval Aviation Safety Center at Norfolk, Virginia, in 1953. A great many records of accidents occurring prior to 1946 are incomplete. The case under discussion is one of them:

At Fort Lauderdale NAS, on the afternoon of December 5, 1945, the day was clear and sunny. There were only a few scattered clouds in the sky.

A flight of five Grumman TBM Avenger torpedo bombers prepared to depart on a routine Coastal Defense System patrol. Known as pregnant fish because of their long underslung torpedo bays, the planes were manned by crews of three—pilot, radioman, and gunner. That day, one crewman had reported to sick bay, so the flight personnel totaled only fourteen.

The day's flight plan called for the patrol to proceed due east for 160 nautical miles, north for 40 miles, and then to return to base. A speed of 215 knots was to be maintained. An International Nautical Mile is a shade over two thousand yards. A knot is the speed of one nautical mile per hour.

Points A, B, and C on the diagram show the flight plan. Estimated time of arrival (ETA) at point B was 1447 hours, and at point C, 1456 hours. The patrol was expected back at NAS Fort Lauderdale at 1542 hours.

The lead plane was airborne at 1402 hours (2:02 P.M.). The fifth plane was six minutes behind it.

At 1545 hours, just about the time the patrol should have radioed in for landing instructions, the control tower received a message from an obviously unnerved flight leader.

"Calling Tower. This is an emergency, Tower. *This is an emergency!*"

"Go ahead."

"We cannot see land. Repeat. *We cannot see land!*"

"What is your position?"

"We are not sure of our position. We can't be sure of where we are. We don't know."

"Assume bearing due west."

"We cannot be sure which way is west. We can't be sure

of any direction. Everything is wrong ... strange. Even the ocean doesn't look as it should!"

The fact that it was impossible to determine which direction was west, as well as that the ocean somehow looked different, has been seized upon as evidence that some dreadfully supernal thing was afoot. If the air was clear, the pilots had only to look for the sun to find the western horizon. Couldn't they see the sun? And just what was wrong with the way the ocean looked?

The control tower at Fort Lauderdale heard the fliers discussing their problem. All testimony from its personnel points up notes of fear, incredulity, and hysteria in the pilots' transmissions. But here an important note is played down, probably by narrators who feel it might spoil a good story (which it does). *The control-tower staff had the distinct impression, from the tempo and tension of the fliers' conversations, that the patrol had been caught up in a blinding storm.*

At 1600 hours, for no clearly ascertainable reason, the lead pilot turned over command of the patrol to another pilot. Not until twenty-five minutes later did the relief pilot call the control tower.

"It is 1625 hours. We are not certain where we are. We seem to be lost. We have enough fuel for 75 more minutes. We must be about 225 miles northeast of base. Looks like we are—"

Transmission ceased abruptly and was never recovered.

At NAS Fort Lauderdale, a giant flying boat, a Martin PBM Mariner, rose into the skies and set forth on a search for the missing patrol. The Mariner, staffed by a crew of thirteen, was especially equipped for rescue work at sea.

The Mariner made a few routine reports and then went silently about its task. But when the control tower tried to contact it at 1930 hours, it did not respond. It was never heard of again.

There is no need to detail the massive search that was launched in the course of the next several days. It has been described elsewhere and has nothing to do with our aspect of the story. I have found that many writers on the case of the missing patrol tend to go into the search details at length, as if they were part of the mystery. They are not.

The actual mystery, as told in a now abundant literature, runs as follows: Five planes, operating in ideal flying conditions on a clear day, suddenly found themselves unable to see the sun or determine direction above an ocean that did not look as it should. Radio contact with them ended abruptly, and no trace of them was ever discovered.

As mysteries go, that's a good one. It is pregnant with the wondrous and with the wondrous it has spawned. Hypotheses advanced to account for it run all the way from holes in space-time, a snatch in midair by a giant mothership UFO, or atmospheric aberrations of a kind that no one seems eager to delineate, down to a possible translation to a planet that does not rotate and hence has an area of perpetual twilight.

If you look closely at the mystery, though, you'll find that tradition has grouped its dots into squares. The telling of the mystery has actually imposed a pattern on it which no true believer is wont to break. I think of a lot of kids tacitly accepting each other's lies rather than spoil a good haunted-house story. Yes, and some adults, too.

Well, let's get to work and break down some of the squares.

One of the misconceptions underlying the mystery seems to stem from the fact that no one likes to chart the movements of the patrol. If you lay out the flight plan on a Hydrographic Office chart, you'll find something that is not mentioned in the narrative accounts.

The first leg of that flight plan took the patrol right into the Bahamas Islands over Northwest Providence Channel. I do not pretend to know what a USN patrol was doing over British waters, since the English had their own air base on New Providence Island. Anyway, if the patrol maintained an altitude of 2,500 feet, its horizon would have had a radius of 67 miles. Before NAS Fort Lauderdale was more than a few miles aft, the Great Isaacs island group would have been on the horizon. (To find your horizon distance, do this. Take 1.3 times the square root of the height of your eye above sea level and express it in miles. That's accurate enough for most navigation purposes.) Minutes later Grand Bahama itself would have appeared to the northeast. From that point on, all the rest of the flight plan would have been by visual fixes—even if the patrol dropped its altitude to 1,000 feet.

Once having turned left at point B, the patrol flew north to point C, located off the east coast of Grand Bahama and below the Little Abaco. The ETA there would be 1456.

The next leg of the course, the return to NAS Fort Lauderdale, would have begun just off and parallel to the southern shoreline of Grand Bahama. For some reason, that course was not pursued.

Now, we *know* that it was not pursued because, had it

31

been, the patrol would not have been out of sight of land, even at a very moderate altitude of 2,500 feet. Now, *why* was the final leg of the course not pursued?

There are many legitimate reasons. The patrol may have wanted to investigate something in the area of point C, for instance. But my opinion is that the fliers were merely extending their mission to accumulate flight-pay time.

During the period when the patrol vanished, it was required that every Navy pilot put in six flying hours each month in order to qualify for his flight-pay bonus. It was preferred that the time be spent on regularly assigned missions, rather than on flights set up purely for the purpose. Frequently, when a mission had sufficient fuel, its flight was extended. The pilots got their time in and nobody was called on the carpet. Any delay that might be questioned was usually covered up by log entries reflecting unexpected weather difficulties.

The patrol's flight was extended, and the matter of flight-pay time seems to me to be the most logical reason.

Where did they go after making good point B? Well, the only open water around lies to the east and to the north. I don't see the patrol flying out to sea with an Avenger's limited fuel capacity—less than 1,000 miles at 215 knots.

A reasonable course would be a simple extension of the point-B–point-C leg of the flight plan. At an altitude of 5,000 feet, Grand Bahama would be visible for 95 miles. At or about that limit, a turn to the left along a course of 270 degrees T would bring the Florida coastline into view before Grand Bahama was out of sight.

It should be noted here that the patrol depended entirely on visual navigation. This was before LORAN and other such navigational aids were in wide use. Celestial navigation served at night, but during the day all you can get out of the sun is a latitude. This may serve to heighten the urgency in the pilot's transmission: "We cannot see land. Repeat. *We cannot see land!*" He was in real trouble, because he needed land configurations to navigate by.

The cause of his trouble is rarely mentioned in accounts of the mystery and, where treated of, is usually glossed over. The facts are these.

Early on December 5, 1945, a great bank of clouds lumbered in from the Gulf of Mexico and rolled across Florida along an axis running from Tampa in the west to Cape Canaveral (now Cape Kennedy, of course) in the east. One of the dots overlooked by writers is that it took three hours

32

for those clouds to make their 140-mile overland trip. In short, *those clouds belonged to a moving mass of air that had a velocity of 40 knots.*

It has been noted that the last of that bank of clouds broke up over the ocean east of Canaveral by 1300 hours. That is meaningless. That says only that the tail end of a cloudbank that had already passed over the horizon had begun to break up and has nothing to do with the velocity of the air mass involved. In fact, at 1600 hours, according to the Miami Weather Bureau, the area east of Canaveral was plagued by freak winds gusting to 40 knots and accompanied by thunderstorms. *That* was the tail end of the air mass.

Where was its front? Right in the way of the patrol coming up from point C.

Now, the speed of a plane is a relative thing. Its *air speed* is the rate at which it moves through the air mass in which it finds itself. Its *land speed* is its actual speed over the ground below. This means that if your air speed is 200 knots and you are in an air mass moving at 25 knots in the other direction, then you make only 200 minus 25, or 175 knots, over the ground, even though your speed indicator reads 200.

Of course, if you don't have any ground to go by, then you have no way of knowing what effect the movement of an air mass is having on your speed.

Now, here is what panicked the lead pilot. On the way north from point C, the patrol entered an air mass moving seaward at the rate of 40 knots. Thus, for every five miles the flight flew north, it was offset to the east by approximately one mile. By the time Grand Bahama is just on the horizon, the patrol had been set off 19 miles seaward. It may have been the shifting position of the Bahamas that first caused a suspicion that something was wrong with the compasses. (I had the same doubts—about my gyrocompass!—the first time I tried to make the Golden Gate at night. The current outside it is not to be believed.)

If the pilot can maintain a 5,000-foot altitude, then, he reasons, he can proceed due west of his assumed position and sight the Florida coastline after traveling 75 miles. But he is unaware that he is 19 miles east of his assumed position and that he will have to cover 94 miles to reach a Florida horizon.

And just to complicate that, he will have to travel at 175 knots, because he will be moving directly into the air mass, and its velocity must be subtracted from his own. Where he assumes that he will sight the Florida coast in twenty-one

33

minutes, he is in error by a factor of about 50 percent, for, under the actual conditions, he cannot make a landfall for thirty-two minutes.

In this illustration, I have used very conservative figures in framing my assumptions. I have assumed the pilot will keep in sight of the Bahamas until he wishes to make his Florida landfall. I have assumed that he will maintain an altitude of 5,000 feet and thus a horizon of 95 miles.

But there is no reason to adhere to those assumptions. It might be that the lead pilot took his patrol far beyond a Bahama horizon by dead reckoning. It may be, particularly in view of the fact he was headed into bad weather, that he was not able to maintain a 5,000-foot altitude. These factors would serve to worsen his situation.

From 1545 to 1600, the pilots, now in the midst of a storm, flew in a careful orientation circle to try to find exactly where they were. By now, though, it is very doubtful if they could maintain even 1,000-foot altitude, and they may even have been wave-hopping.

Now, here's something to gladden a publisher's heart; a little cause for contention. It has to do with group navigational practice in the USN. Optimally, when a group of planes or ships is out on an exercise involving navigation, it follows the courses as laid down by the OTC—he's the Officer in Tactical Command, the leader. But it is expected that each unit of the group do its own navigation—the idea being that if one unit gets separated from the rest, it won't be lost.

It doesn't always happen that way in real life. In a real-life situation involving a pretty routine mission, the units sometimes let the navigation slide, depending on the OTC's to see them through. And, as a rule, this works out all right.

But then you get the navigation buff. He's the officer that always has to be taking fixes on things, working out maneuvering-board problems, and harassing communicators to cut in WWV so he can get a time check for his Longines Chronograph. I think the flier to whom the flight leader surrendered command at 1600 hours was one of these. My reason for thinking so is that he gave what was apparently a pretty good 1625 hours position—225 miles northeast of NAS Fort Lauderdale. If you follow my reasoning in the above paragraphs and look at the diagram, you'll see that that was pretty close to where we could expect him to be.

Only a dyed-in-the-wool navigation buff would have done that. He would have had to base his calculations on a meticulous logging of every single maneuver, air speeds, and apparent offset of visual reference points. When he attributed such offsets to the movement of an air mass and not confused compasses, he was on the right track. But he was too late.

One of the squares that separate our mystery from solution is the fact that nobody ever had the slightest clue as to what happened to the five planes. This is not entirely true. We can break that square down into the following dots.

0200 hours, December 8, 1945. Captain J. D. Morrison, pilot of a northbound Eastern Airlines flight, reported seeing red flares and flashing lights in the middle of a swamp ten miles southwest of Melbourne, Florida. He said he saw figures standing in the light of the flares.

0205 hours, same date. Captain Morrison reported seeing a fire burning in an area twenty miles north of the first sighting.

0230 hours, same date. The pilot of a Navy plane dispatched from NAS Banana River to investigate Captain Morrison's reports said that he also observed a fire burning about fifty miles inland.

By dawn of that date, however, a heavy fog had rolled into the area and made further search by plane impossible. A search carried out on land and swamp by marsh buggies, DUKW's, and other craft proved fruitless.

January 1962. An American magazine, *The Searcher,* picked up the following from a Netherlands source: Plane wreckage and human bones were found recently in dredging operations in Banana River. Though the remains were apparently not in sufficient quantity to afford conclusive evidence of having come from the lost patrol, considered in the light of the Morrison and Navy sightings, they do suggest an air tragedy in the area.*

The relief patrol leader, in his last communication, reported that the planes had enough fuel for 75 more minutes of operation. At the cruising speed of 215 knots, that would have produced 270 miles over ground. However, for a patrol that was heading into an air mass with a velocity of 40 knots, the overground distance made good would be only 219 miles.

If we draw a 219-mile circle on our diagram with its center at a point common to the Morrison sightings and the Banana River find, we find that its circumference passes through the very area at which we found the Avengers to be

---

*I am indebted to independent researcher George Wagner of Fort Thomas, Kentucky, for bringing the Banana River find to my attention in a private communication.

in trouble. We also find that that point is just about due east of the center of the circle.

I think that the last, interrupted sentence of the relief flight leader was intended to be, "Looks like we are *going to have to put in at Banana River.*" He knew he could not make NAS Fort Lauderdale, but he probably did not know of the thunderstorms that the Miami Weather Bureau was to report off Banana River.

In December 1961, Captain E. W. Humphrey, USN, Coordinator of Aviation Safety, made a statement about the missing planes. While insisting that what he had to say was conjecture and unsupported by factual evidence, he said: "Strong westerly winds prevail in the wintertime over the northern hemisphere, and the flight of aircraft may have proceeded farther to sea than planned, having insufficient fuel to return. Radio communications equipment did not have the range of present-day equipment and may have precluded communication of difficulties encountered."

If the planes moved overland in a windy, rainy dusk and pancaked in the swamps of central Florida, why weren't they seen? Well, how do we know they *weren't* seen? They might well have been seen—but not *noticed*. Residents of Melbourne and Melbourne Beach, the areas in which the planes probably came in from the sea, would have no more reason to notice a group of low-flying planes than they would any of the many routine flights associated with the Banana River NAS.

Were they picked up on NAS Banana River radar? Probably, and if they were flying low, just as probably dismissed as aberrances in the welter of "sea return" that the radar operators were getting from the wind-whipped waters off Canaveral.

Why weren't they found in the swamps? Have you ever been in one of those Florida swamps? And in a fog, too. Those are flatland swamps. The highest point in the whole state of Florida is only 325 feet above sea level. In such a swamp, beset by fog, you are in a strange, dimensionless land with no reliable reference points. Instead, you have quicksand, tarantulas, alligators, and snakes that can kill with almost the suddenness of electrocution.

Once while proceeding through swampy terrain, the officer with me reached for what he thought was a hanging vine. It bit him. He turned to me with eyes and mouth wide open but didn't utter a sound. The hospital corpsman with us had antivenin and saved him. Later he told me, "When it hit me, it

36

felt like a hammer blow. Everything started to get dark at once. It was as if an iron band was around my chest. If I had had to yell for help, I couldn't have."

There is also the matter of hunger and exposure. . . .

Shouldn't there have been fire and smoke where the planes pancaked? Not with empty gas tanks.

What about the automatic Gibson Girl radio transmitter? That's the kind you hold between your knees. Turn a crank, and it belts out its own coded signal. Fine in a liferaft with an unobstructed sea; not so good on land. Then, you have to get it out of the plane, too—something that may be a little hard to remember if the craft is settling in a swamp lake or quicksand.

Let's put together a summary hypothesis based on what we have seen so far.

A five-plane patrol set out from NAS Fort Lauderdale under clear skies and over a relatively smooth sea. It was to follow a simple flight plan on which it was guided by visual points of reference.

When it completed the second leg of its flight, it proceeded farther in a northerly direction, for reasons that seemed justified to its members.

As it so proceeded, it entered a strong and rapidly moving air mass that had crossed Florida earlier in the day. This forced the patrol seaward and caused confusion about visual compass bearings. The flight leader believed the compasses were at fault.

An attempt to make a dead-reckoning landfall on the Florida coast was frustrated by an erroneous assumed position and a failure to understand the actual velocity of the moving air mass. An overcast obscured the sun and complicated the problem.

The flight leader surrendered command to an officer who had, apparently, kept a careful track of the patrol's progress. The relief leader calculated what seems to have been a close approximation of the patrol's position and proceeded on a 270-degree T course in the hope of reaching NAS Banana River.

Thunderstorms and turbulence off Cape Canaveral as well as exhausted fuel supply prevented his doing this.

Of the planes, at least three pancaked in the swampland east of Melbourne. One other pancaked into the Banana River—actually a thirty-mile-long banana-shaped lagoon that separates Merritt Island from the Canaveral Peninsula. This plane may have been flipped over into the lagoon by atmospheric turbulence, particularly if its engine was out of fuel. In that case, it would have plunged to the bottom instantly.

When the lead pilot reported that the ocean did not look as it should, he gave evidence that the patrol was farther seaward than he believed. The shallow continental-shelf waters off Florida have a much lighter appearance than the 2,000-foot-deep Gulf Stream over which he found himself flying. Normally a beautiful blue, the waters of the Gulf Stream take on a dark and ominous color under a heavy overcast.

There is one other matter we want to consider here—that of the Mariner flying boat.

The problem of the Mariner is usually grouped with the matter of the Avengers in one mystery. There is no reason why it should be. There is nothing to link it with the Avengers except the fact that it was looking for them. It is true that its last contact with NAS Fort Lauderdale was a routine report made about twenty minutes after it took off. This is sometimes construed to mark the point in time when it vanished. That point is groundless. Standard military usage discourages negative reports. That is, if you're looking for something and don't find it, you don't keep calling your base to advertise your failure. Your base wants to hear when you get results.

At 1950 hours on December 5, the SS *Gaines Mills*, making its way along the Florida coast an easy distance off New Smyrna Beach, saw an explosion high in the sky and to seaward. It saw what looked like a plane spin into the sea.

Farmers from Melbourne to Orlando reported hearing an explosion at what seems to have been the same time.

The *Gaines Mills* couldn't pinpoint the location of the explosion, and apparently didn't even report it until a couple of days after it happened. Search planes moved into the appropriate area could find no debris or gasoline slicks. It would have been strange if they had: the Gulf Stream would have carried them at least two hundred miles away by then. If a plane crashes in flames, its gasoline slick doesn't last any longer than it takes to burn out, though a few traces of lubricating oil may remain.

In the absence of any other reports of missing planes at the time, it may be presumed that the explosion seen by the *Gaines Mills* represented the end of the Mariner. Why the Mariner should explode in midair is another problem.

The explosion could not have been one of the Avengers,

because, as we have seen, they would have been out of gas two hours before it happened.

What we have done here is to take a single Bermuda Triangle case and, by closely examining its elements in the light of common sense, stripped from it all vestiges of the paranormal. What remains, though it may be open to criticism around the edges, is more credible than explanations based on "holes in the sky" or a hypothetical kinkiness in space-time.

Paranormal events do occur, and I'm sure that a lot of them have occurred in the Bermuda Triangle, but the only way we are ever going to be able to separate the truly strange events from the merely apparently weird is to take them out of the hands of the miracle mongers and pile them on the desks of the boys with the charts and slide rules.

5. Public Mystery Number One— Or Just a Hoax?

An interview with Lawrence David Kusche

by Wanda Sue Parrott

Lawrence David Kusche, research librarian at the Hayden Library of Arizona State University in Tempe, is probably the most meticulously informed student of the Bermuda Triangle. In his book The Bermuda Triangle Mystery—Solved *(Harper & Row, 1975), he examined the evidence behind the often flamboyant claims made by others concerning the circumstances and possible causes of ships, planes, and people that have disappeared in the area. Kusche received a B.A. in mathematics from Arizona State University in 1964, an M.A. in secondary education, also from ASU, in 1966, and the degree of Master of Library Science from the University of Denver in 1968. In his book, Kusche concluded that "the Legend of the Bermuda Triangle is a manufactured mystery," in which "careless research," use of "misconceptions, faulty reasoning, and sensationalism" played a role.*

Wanda Sue Parrott, as a reporter and columnist with The Los Angeles Herald-Examiner *from 1968 to 1974, specialized in science, education, and psychology, including, as she puts it, "an offbeat educational accent on parapsychology." Her scientific interests began as a high-school senior, when she installed a full-fledged weather-forecasting station in her parents' home. Her writings, under her own name and pseudonyms, have appeared in* Fate, Chimes, *and* Orion. *Her first book,* Understanding Automatic Writing, *was published in 1974. She now lives in Tempe, Arizona, engaged in writing and filmmaking.*

Is THE Bermuda Triangle mystery a hoax? Did writers and reporters draw inaccurate conclusions from reference materials used as the bases of their stories, thus creating a strange myth about vanishing boats, planes, and people?

The Bermuda Triangle, Public Mystery Number One in mid-1970's American history, is purportedly a triangular zone of Atlantic Ocean waters, ranging roughly from Miami, Florida, north to Bermuda and south past the Bahama Islands, West Indies, Guadeloupe, and Barbados. In this watery grave more than one hundred craft have been reported as having disappeared mysteriously in the past century. More than one thousand lives have been lost.

If there is a solution to the mystery, it is also evident that the mass public mind created multitudes of mental cults around the Bermuda Triangle mystery, basing its beliefs on concepts such as these: extraterrestrials or ancient astronauts have visited our planet and established earth bases, and modern craft passing through these areas disappear as if into space; power sources from sunken ancient Atlantis are responsible for the disappearances. Many supporters of the Bermuda Triangle cult have a quasi-religious adherence to it. Others see the issue as a political conflict: in one arena the believers, in the other corner the nonbelievers.

Is there an answer for those in the middle, the men and women who neither believe passionately nor disbelieve, just as passionately, in the Bermuda Triangle mystery? They, too, are intrigued by it and by the question: Is it really Public Mystery Number One?

In an attempt to determine an objective answer to the above question, I visited the center of bibliographical information about the Bermuda Triangle and talked with

Lawrence David Kusche, author of *The Bermuda Triangle Mystery—Solved* (Harper & Row, 1975). Ironically, Kusche lives and works in the center of the arid Arizona desert, more than two thousand miles from the purportedly treacherous waters that made him one of "America's leading experts on the Bermuda Triangle."

I visited Kusche on the Arizona State University campus, where he had worked as science reference librarian for six years, in the first half of 1975.

The modern, compact campus was a true oasis of green and brick in an otherwise dry, dusty, and naturally magnetic Valley of the Sun.

The campus of ASU is nested beneath a sharply pointed series of dark purple hills called Tempe Butte, north of which the famed Camelback Mountain stands as the dominant silent overseer of the valley. Near the camel stands another rock formation known as "the monk." The land is flat in Tempe on ASU's 330-acre campus, where more than 30,000 students attend day and night classes and where Lawrence David Kusche did his research on the Bermuda Triangle mystery.

This was not my first visit to the campus, although it was a first-time trip to Hayden Library. I had come to the Phoenix area in the fall of 1974 to complete research and writing of *Auras* for Sherbourne Press. The forty-square-mile section of Arizona, centered around Phoenix, was truly a psychic center in America. My own research had proven that though it was a psychic center (with more practicing psychics, ministers, witches, soothsayers, drug cultists, etc., in a concentrated area than in most metropolitan centers), it was *not* a center for genuine psychic research. That is, while thousands of men and women could discuss "truth" or practice ESP, palmistry, astrology, aura reading, and healing with amazing facility, few could explain how and why these principles worked. They accepted on faith many "truths," with the result being that we found that many of the so-called psychic circles of truth were diversely split. I concluded that science was a threat, not a boon, to many of these so-called enlightened persons. Would I discover that Lawrence David Kusche was another well-meaning but misdirected "psychic opportunist" spawned in the Valley of the Sun?

Like the Hayden Library, Lawrence David Kusche looked clean, new, as he stood behind a glass partition discussing a blue-jeaned student's research problems. He is a crisply bearded, short-haired man of trim, athletic firmness, slightly under six feet tall, in his mid-thirties. He greeted me with a handshake, not warmly and not coolly. Appraisingly. Kusche's dark brown eyes looked directly into my own eyes from behind black-framed glasses that highlighted the burnt-sienna tones of his hair and beard. Throughout the interview he would look directly at me when he spoke, a feat many psychics and purported experts in various fields never achieve. "Call me Larry," he said. "That's what I'm known by." A small identification badge on the left lapel of his long-sleeved brown pullover shirt distinguished him from the students, a few of whom were older than the reference librarian.

Throughout the interview Larry Kusche said, "Excuse me," and would turn to help students locate materials ranging from child-psychology abstracts to Bermuda Triangle articles. He made no issue of the fact that he had authored, with another ASU librarian, the very material to which he directed students when they queried about the Triangle. He emphasized, in fact, "My purpose in compiling the material was to help students find what they needed." His Bermuda Triangle Bibliography was begun in 1972, "after students kept asking for information and there was none to be found." He worked in his spare time and on weekends to compile the bibliography of Bermuda Triangle material. In 1973 the project was completed. Orders were received from the general public, scientific-research organizations, and libraries across the country.

"At that time I realized a book needed to be written," Kusche told me. "I intended originally to do a book that told of the major incidents that make up the Bermuda Triangle mystery, like an anthology." The next year, several books did appear, and a film about the Triangle was shown around the country. By the end of 1974 the Bermuda Triangle was unquestionably Public Mystery Number One. And Kusche, whose own form of research included digging through old newspapers for originally published stories about the Triangle incidents, discovered that the stories as told during the twentieth century often digressed greatly from the factual reports that appeared in nineteenth-century newspapers.

Thus, his book manuscript, being completed under contract with Harper & Row, took a form different from others published about the Bermuda Triangle. Kusche incorporated the legends as popularly told and retold, included factual accounts as he discovered them in his research, and listed bibliographical sources of material quoted in the book.

"I did not set out to debunk anyone's theories," Kusche repeated, emphasizing his belief that the mystery has many sides. "I don't want to sound like I'm trying to make what other writers have said sound bad. But after all this research, my opinion is that all the previous books only scratch the surface. There was a genuine need for a book of this type."

As Kusche's fame as "the Bermuda Triangle expert" spread, he became a subject of numerous interviews and radio talk shows. Kusche grew uncertain how his life would be affected: "What kind of man am I? Well, I guess you could call me middle-class. I have one wife, two kids, one dog, and one 1964 Pontiac that I might have repainted when I get some royalties from my book."

Kusche rides his three-speed bicycle to work. "I live two miles from campus," he said. "In the six years I've worked here I've probably ridden five thousand miles. I work out on the half-mile track every day, too. I run between five and ten miles a day."

He has never been to the actual Bermuda Triangle mystery site. "Arizona is my world," he said.

Following are questions and answers about that mystery, recorded during my interview with Lawrence David Kusche on February 12, 1975:

WSP: You claim your work differs from all others written about the Bermuda Triangle mystery. Why is this?

KUSCHE: It's a solution. It is an objective look at all the information I was able to find. Each incident was examined extensively, and independently of all the others, and as a result, I found the solution.

WSP: If it's not really a mystery, are you suggesting it's a hoax?

KUSCHE: Previous writers, either on purpose or because they were gullible, created the mystery. I found that many things writers call mysterious really aren't if you take the trouble to dig for some information. Previous writers on this topic had to be either very poor researchers with little curiosity, very gullible, or outright sensationalists. They've been passing off their own lack of information as mysteries.

WSP: You take a bold stand. Do you think people will believe your solution to the Bermuda Triangle mystery, or do you think they will refuse to believe you because you are taking away their belief in something paranormal, or supernatural?

KUSCHE: If this is an example of the paranormal, then I'd say the paranormal business is about to go bankrupt. Between October 1974 and February 1975 I spoke to many school and civic groups, possibly to about seven thousand people, and only one person really hit the nail on the head. He asked, "Has anybody ever checked to see if what the previous authors said about the mystery is true?" Everyone else asked fairy-tale questions like, "Do you think the ancient astronauts are responsible?" or "Are UFO's capturing them?" They accepted all the "facts" they had been handed, then tried to find a solution based on that erroneous information.

The ancient-astronaut nonsense and psychic solutions for the Triangle mystery are pure sensationalism.

Most people don't go very heavily into these subjects. They read the popular, one-sided books (or sometimes they just "learn" it by hearsay, not even bothering to read the books) and only scratch the surface. I found that although everyone I spoke to "knew" about the Bermuda Triangle, most had it only by hearsay. They hadn't taken the time to question any of it.

WSP: How did your book come about?

KUSCHE: It began early in 1972 when students at Arizona State University kept asking for material on the Bermuda Triangle and there was none to be found.

Another reference librarian, Deborah Blouin, and I decided to make a list of all the articles we could find. We worked about six months on it, writing letters and doing research. I then realized that someone should accumulate all the various articles and publish it as a book, because there was none at the time. *Limbo of the Lost* wasn't too well known then. We made the bibliography available and found that everyone seemed to be having trouble finding information, because we were swamped with requests, including orders from John Wallace Spencer, Richard Winer, and Charles Berlitz. Harper & Row also ordered one, and I sent a note along, telling them I was writing a book. They offered me a contract based on two sample chapters.

I had started writing early in 1973, and Harper & Row originally planned to have the book out by April 1974. This would have been five months before the Berlitz book, *The Bermuda Triangle*, which, of course, we didn't know about then. I had originally gotten hold of accounts by previous writers, threw them all together, and put a few transition sentences between them. That's the twenty percent of my book that's in italics.

I departed from this original plan because I began to see signs that it was all more a lack of information rather than a real mystery that anyone had tried to solve.

As I really dug into it, it became more difficult, not only the research and writing, but also the printing problems for the publisher. As a result, it took an extra year to get the book published.

WSP: Don't you feel that the different books about the Bermuda Triangle cause people to pause and think? For instance, John Wallace Spencer concludes in *Limbo of the Lost* that extraterrestrial craft are responsible for the strange disappearances of ships and planes in the Triangle. You take a different view.

KUSCHE: I wouldn't call any book a "think book" if it is one-sided, works toward confirming a preconceived conclusion, and fails to tell where the information came from.

Most people I've talked to thought they were doing creative thinking ("stretching their minds" is the current cliché), but all I ever heard was a regurgitation of one-liners from Berlitz, Von Däniken, and the rest of the gang.

I feel *my* book is thought-provoking because it presents another side of the topic for the first time. If any "pausing and thinking" ever takes place on this subject, it'll start with the information I present. It came from Coast Guard, Navy, and Lloyd's of London reports, as well as from the original accounts about the vessels that "disappeared" as reported in the newspapers at the time.

I also searched *The New York Times* for ship and plane losses from 1851 to the present and found at least twice as many disappearances between New England and Northern Europe as in the Bermuda Triangle. These were ignored or probably not even seen by writers of the mystery. It's more fun and a lot easier and quicker to write a mystery than to find out what really happened.

Ignorance of the subject is a great advantage to a pseudo-scientific mystery writer.

WSP: Do you believe writers deliberately set out to perpetrate a hoax?

KUSCHE: Many of the writers probably believe what they wrote. I believed what they said until I had checked into it for a while.

Most of the writers accepted what others wrote and then built on it. The story of the *Ellen Austin*, for instance, tells of a ship that was found in the mid-Atlantic. The crew was gone. A salvage crew from the *Ellen Austin* boarded the ship and then disappeared during a thick fog. A second salvage crew then went aboard, and this time, ship and crew disappeared during a storm. That's the story that's usually told. As far as I could discover, it didn't really happen that way, but other writers accepted that version and repeated it.

I did my research on the *Ellen Austin* by borrowing newspapers on microfilm through the Interlibrary Loan Department at Arizona State University. First I borrowed the *Newfoundlander,* from St. John's, since that was the supposed destination of the *Ellen Austin.* I searched that paper day by day, every column of every page, from January 1881 through June 1882. There were several articles about incidents at sea, but nothing about the *Ellen Austin* or any similar incident that involved a ship by any other name. If the event had really happened and the ship had gone to St. John's, it's extremely unlikely the paper would have missed printing it.

I wrote several Newfoundland newspapers and libraries and asked if they could check their files. They couldn't find anything either.

After all that, Richard Winer's book, *The Devil's Triangle,* came out and said the ship's destination was Boston. I repeated the whole process, borrowing microfilm, contacting newspapers and libraries, and searching more microfilm. There wasn't a trace of the story in Boston either.

WSP: From where did the story come, if that's possible to answer?

KUSCHE: Like many of the other stories, the main source is Vincent Gaddis' book *Invisible Horizons.* Gaddis cited Rupert Gould's *The Stargazer Talks* as his only source; Gould had one brief paragraph about the *Ellen Austin.* He said it was found abandoned in the mid-Atlantic and a salvage crew was put on board. The ships parted during a heavy fog but met several days later, and the derelict was deserted again. Gould's account ends there. He didn't say anything about a second salvage crew, and he didn't tell where he got his information, although I'm currently borrowing, through Interlibrary Loan again, an earlier book that supposedly mentions it. I'm hoping maybe it will lead somewhere.

WSP: Gould's version is not the popular one. People believe two salvage crews disappeared.

KUSCHE: Gaddis gave his source of information as Gould, yet Gaddis' account has a lot of "information" that wasn't in Gould's account.

Then, Ivan Sanderson came along, citing both Gould and Gaddis. Sanderson's version in *Invisible Residents* went on for a full page. You'd think he had actually been there, the way he described it. He was very creative.

Berlitz relies very heavily on Sanderson in his *The Bermuda Triangle*. Winer went even further! He talks about the captain of the *Ellen Austin* motioning his men forward with his Colt revolver, listening to the creaking of the ship and the slamming of the galley door, and squashing a cockroach as he boarded the derelict. Maybe he was practicing for *Moby-Dick II*.

WSP: Did you intend to debunk any myths or take away anyone's belief in God, no matter that it might have been a false-god concept based on the idea that the Bermuda Triangle gave evidence of supernatural powers?

KUSCHE: I don't see any kind of god in all this. Also, I dislike the word "debunk," because it carries the connotation that someone set out to prove someone else wrong, which was not what I did. My purpose, throughout, was not even to find a solution but merely to write a book that reported each incident as objectively and honestly as possible. The solution was completely unintentional and was an added bonus.

I found I couldn't trust anything anybody else had written on the topic, because it was very flimsy.

Many vessels that supposedly disappeared in the Triangle did not disappear anywhere near it.

One of the planes, a Globemaster, reportedly vanished "just north" of the Triangle in 1950. I found an account of the incident in *The New York Times*. The plane had exploded in 1951, not 1950, six hundred miles west of Ireland, which is really stretching the Triangle a bit.

The *Freya*, according to stories, was found mysteriously abandoned in the Triangle in 1902. In real life, it had been found in the Pacific Ocean near Mazatlán, Mexico.

The *Rubicon* was found drifting off the coast of Florida in 1944. There was only one article on the ship in *The New York Times*, and it told not only about the discovery of the ship but also about the hurricane that had struck Havana, where the *Rubicon* had been moored. The hurricane had mysteriously disappeared from the accounts of all writers, except Winer.

I found, time after time, that fairly simple reasons could account for the losses. The most important question, then, is "How and why did the mystery get to be so big?" and I am trying to analyze how the story was born, nourished, and grew. To me, it's far more interesting than either the Bermuda Triangle mystery or the solution, because it has applications in related fields.

There's a whole subculture of pseudo-scientific mystery writers that have been pumping out this kind of material on ancient astronauts, UFO's, the Bermuda Triangle, and other topics for many years, without opposition of any kind. I plan to bring my bulldozer in and show that their buildings aren't concrete, but just bubbles and baubles piled high and deep.

WSP: What did you find out about airplanes that disappeared in the Bermuda Triangle, specifically the six military planes in 1945?

KUSCHE: Flight 19 was a complicated affair, but there was nothing mysterious about it except the writing that later described it. Much of the so-called occult field consists of poor research piled on top of poor research. Somebody will quote from an incomplete newspaper article; then the next writer comes along and quotes the first one, not bothering to check the original source. Then the third one quotes (or misquotes, or adds to) the second one and says it's factual and documented.

My solution to the Bermuda Triangle mystery is relevant to the entire "occult" or "pseudo-science" field, because it will be obvious that many of these writers are not really reporting mysteries that exist, but are creating the mysteries.

WSP: If the Bermuda Triangle mystery lies in the realm of pseudo-science or fringe-science, why have bona-fide scientists not found the facts and released their conclusions to a curious—or is it gullible—public?

KUSCHE: They've learned over the years that it doesn't pay to fight this sort of thing. The circulation of the sensational material is much higher than the scientific writings. Most people never even hear of any material that gives a contradictory view. Knowing that a refutation wouldn't get very far anyway, legitimate scientists don't concern themselves with going around explaining incomplete newspaper articles. Back in the 1920's Charles Fort wrote books that "science dare not answer." Much of what he said were just ramblings, based on a vast collection of excerpts from newspaper articles that had been accepted at face value, with absolutely no follow-up.

WSP: What happened to all those ships and planes, and why were they never found?

KUSCHE: They sank in deep water.

WSP: Have you ever flown over or taken a boat ride through the Bermuda Triangle?

KUSCHE: No. I live in Arizona and have never been anywhere near the Bermuda Triangle, although I shall certainly go there. This was a historical study, on both my part and that of the previous writers. There was nothing to be gained by going to the area to do the research. The material I found through Interlibrary Loan, by mail, and by telephone is the very same material I'd have asked for if I'd gone in person. Taking a ride through the Triangle would be no help to anyone wanting to know what happened to Flight 19, thirty years ago, for example.

The writers who created the mystery apparently didn't benefit from being near the Triangle, because the purpose of their writing was to let everyone know how confused they were by it all.

Now, I like a mystery just like everyone does, but I can tell the difference between what's factual and what's only half-factual. If we could separate the half-fact information from the good, we might be able to take a hard, honest look at such topics as UFO's, extraterrestrial visits to this planet, and the Bermuda Triangle. As it is now, there's so much interference from sensationalists that the good information, if there is any, is hidden.

49

Many people operate only on the hearsay level of knowledge, and they are often willing to argue endlessly with someone who has good information. The hearsayists are the greatest of critics, seeking flaws in others' explanations, yet not doing a bit of research or even reading themselves. I found that many of the people who attempted to argue the most with me (I prefer to discuss, not argue) hadn't ever read the books that told the "mystery" of the Triangle. As a result of their lack of knowledge, they make up or believe "explanations" such as UFO's or death rays from Atlantis, and it never occurs to them that, maybe, there is a very simple explanation.

The information I assembled is very solid, and those who refuse to believe it ought to ask themselves why they don't. Do they disbelieve the sources I found, or do they just want to cling to the "mystery" regardless of whatever contradictory information they see? As the proverb I recently made up goes, "If your eyes are always on the horizon, you probably won't see what's directly in front of your nose."

In a follow-up interview with Lawrence David Kusche on February 20, 1975, I performed a little experiment to determine if he truly was a man of his word—open-minded enough to listen to others' views while retaining his own convictions. He, of course, was unaware that I was attempting to "trick" him. "May I see your palms?" I asked, and he complied. I told him a few personal things, based on popular concepts of palmistry as practiced widely in the Valley of the Sun, concluding with the tracing of one tiny but long line that reached his little finger.

"That line indicates that very soon you will make a lot of money," I said.

There was a pause. Then silence. After a moment Larry Kusche smiled and said with quiet dignity, "I like what you're saying, but it's only fair to tell you that I don't believe a word of it."

6. Edgar Cayce and the Search for Atlantis

by David D. Zink

Can the clairvoyant impressions or retrospective views of Edgar Cayce, the most prominent American seer of this century, help to clarify the mystery of the Bermuda Triangle? Dr. David Zink, who is currently professor of English at Lamar University, Beaumont, Texas, has made a special study of such frontier research areas as Kirlian photography, parapsychological studies generally, Atlantis, mystical experience, the evolution of human consciousness, and his own philosophy of personality, "psychointegration."

THE LOGICAL point of departure from which to suggest a connection between the Atlantis topic and the Bermuda Triangle is the Edgar Cayce material, ten million words on file at the Association for Research and Enlightenment (ARE), Virginia Beach, Virginia. Despite the mounting evidence within parapsychology for the validity of the work of authentic psychics like the late prophet and clairvoyant Edgar Cayce, I recognize that clairvoyant information developed through psychic channels is as yet highly suspect in scientific circles. Nonetheless, faced by the mind-boggling phenomena of the Bermuda Triangle, the Western mind is now being forced to consider even more bizarre possibilities.

The Cayce version of Atlantis developed from twenty-five hundred trance-state psychic readings that apparently described one or more previous lifetimes for about sixteen hundred people. These readings were done between October 11, 1923, and January 3, 1945. In them the rise of Atlantis, its golden age, and its final destruction were traced with these by now well-known features: great stone cities; modern communications, including electronics; land, air, and undersea transportation; the neutralization of gravity; harnessing the sun's energy through "fire stones," and transmission of power to air, land, and water vehicles at a distance from the fire stones. According to the Cayce readings, misuse of these

51

crystals (*i.e.*, technology) caused at least one of the cataclysmic events which triggered the tectonic activity that destroyed Atlantis.

Aside from the exotic technology of Cayce's Atlantis, his account of spirits descending into matter and finally being trapped is consistent with Plato and consistent with a follower of Plato in the early Christian centuries, Plotinus. Among other shocks that Cayce himself sustained (as a fundamentalist Christian) from his readings was the stunning idea that the first incarnation of the Christ consciousness, Amelius, appeared on Atlantis.

From its golden age, in the Cayce readings, Atlantis deteriorated through materialism, sexual perversion and exploitation, and slavery. This decline was marked by a sharpening conflict between the Sons of the Law of One and the Sons of Belial. (This may remind the reader of the Sons of Light and the Sons of Darkness of the Dead Sea Scrolls.) The latter, the Sons of Belial, degenerated into human sacrifice, sexual license, including psychic control of others for sexual exploitation, and finally the misuse of the forces of nature, particularly through the fire stones, which earlier had also been used for healing, later for punishment and torture. This may represent the beginning of black magic. Aside from these exotic details, the moral decline parallels Plato and a variety of other accounts of Atlantis based on psychic sources.

The Atlanteans, many of whom Cayce saw incarnated in the twentieth century, were extremists, desiring greatly either to serve mankind or to exploit others. Cayce saw that many had an individual or group karma involving exploitation of others, representing individual debts which have yet to be worked out. The Cayce readings on Atlantis are conveniently available in a book by one of his sons. Edgar Evans Cayce, *Edgar Cayce on Atlantis* (1968).

Cayce's trance-state life readings, because of their usefulness to individuals laboring under physical and mental difficulties, are taken seriously by those who consult the evidence, as did the author of *Many Mansions* (1950), Dr. Gina Cerminara. But whether or not the readings prove reincarnation, or merely a collective unconscious, will not be argued here. Either hypothesis (and others) logically follows from the evidence and its effect on individual lives. On the other hand, the Cayce readings contain predictions about the "rediscovery" of Atlantean technology which have begun to seem prophetic.

One of Cayce's readings that was set in the Atlantean context, a reading dated February 21, 1933, speaks of a "death ray" used anciently, which was to be discovered again in twenty-five years. In 1957 antineutrons were produced in a laboratory, which led to the theoretical possibility of building up "antimatter" that would have a far greater destructive potential than nuclear fission or fusion reactions. In 1958 the Bell laboratories developed the maser and, later, the laser, one type of which uses the ruby, as did the alleged "fire crystal" on Atlantis. As yet, of course, the destructive power of these devices is relatively small.

To develop a working hypothesis about the Bermuda Triangle, then, let us assume that the Cayce readings do in fact describe an actual prehistoric civilization whose remaining artifacts may include the so-called "fire crystal"—possibly in a latent condition, possibly randomly triggered. Let us also assume that Cayce's geographical location, near Bimini, is also valid. What we have so far, then, is the possibility of an ancient power source drawing on solar energy as a possible explanation of the mysterious disappearances and electromagnetic anomalies experienced by small vessels and aircraft traversing the Triangle. These anomalies, including erratic compasses, radio and ignition failures, have been painstakingly collected by my friend Dr. J. Manson Valentine of Miami. They appear in Charles Berlitz' *The Bermuda Triangle* (1974).

The ancient-power-source hypothesis is not inconsistent with Ivan Sanderson's efforts, in *Invisible Residents* (1970), to describe anomalies, even gravitational ones, in areas of the earth's surface where hot tropical seas jet with a relatively narrow current into colder seas. If Atlantis actually existed, perhaps its inhabitants had a much better attunement with the forces of nature than do we, at least until their last days. If so, their location of a power source may not have been accidental.

Finally, one psychic whose work so far seems valid has suggested (in a reading done for me) that the Bahamas represent an area of the earth's surface from which spontaneous access to parallel universes is possible. Again, this is not inconsistent with the Atlantean possibility *or* contemporary speculation about those reported UFO phenomena which seem to point to parallel universes with different time and space characteristics.

These speculations should give the reader some idea of the possible implications of the Bimini area. Before we get down to the specifics of the expedition itself, I would like to make clear (1) the meaning of Atlantis for me as a historian of ideas and (2) my position on the use of paranormally derived information for the construction of archaeological hypotheses.

In the 1960's, when I thought about the Atlantis idea, I still considered it Plato's moralizing. Then, in 1967, A. G. Galanapoulos began to claim that he had found Atlantis, not in the Atlantic, but in the Aegean, on the island of Santorini. Later this claim was detailed in his book, *Atlantis; the Truth Behind the Legend* (1972). Shortly after, I encountered the Cayce material and, almost simultaneously, heard of the discovery at Bimini apparently predicted by Cayce. These events caused me to wonder if, like many legends, Atlantis might not be ready for a now-not-uncommon metamorphosis in the history of ideas: the change of status from legend to archaeological fact. It had earlier happened for Troy, Pompeii, the Seven Cities of Cibola (in South America), the Well of Sacrifice at Chichén Itzá in the Yucatán, and King Arthur and his knights. Paralleling these developments, a new geology was beginning to emerge which was somewhat more hospitable to dramatic earth changes in the past, even to the cataclysmic theories of Immanual Velikovsky, particularly since some of his claims had been verified by the probes of the space program.

Unless those trained in the spirit of Victorian uniformitarian geology could admit that the earth might have experienced widespread catastrophic events, the possible sinking of Atlantis would remain a nonsubject. The recent worldwide voyages of the *Glomar Challenger,* whose cores drilled in the world's ocean beds seem conclusive evidence of continental drift, also turned up evidence of a very impressive geological event. Sediments in the Mediterranean, because they contain marine fossils of life forms usually deep in the Atlantic, tell of a dramatic ancient opening of the Strait of Gibraltar which poured the Atlantic into a tropical valley. These and other discoveries of the new geology increase the geological plausibility of the Atlantis story. These developments in the history of ideas all began to make me realize that Atlantis was a substantial archaeological possibility.

The second point to clarify before going on to Bimini is the basis for my use of ESP in projects of an archaeological nature. As a historian of ideas, I have studied the phenomena associated with the traditional mystical experience for fifteen years, the experience recently labeled "ultraconsciousness" by the Miami psychiatrist Dr. Stanley R. Dean. Dr. Dean sees important medical implications in the experience. About five years ago this research led me into serious work in parapsychology at my university. I have concentrated on paranormal healing, clairvoyance, and psychometry. The paranormal healing led me, with the help of the UCLA physiologist Dr. Thelma Moss, to establish a Kirlian-photography project three years ago at Lamar University. All this work has given me enough of a feeling for both the validity and the nature of paranormal phenomena that I have come to regard paranormal data as plausible bases for hypotheses about both prehistorical problems and archaeological investigations. In some cases such data have proven to be entirely misleading. In other cases they have been very fruitful. They must therefore be used with caution; they cannot be disregarded.

The earliest events which point to Bimini as a possible Atlantean site are two of Edgar Cayce's readings on Atlantis. In 1933 the first of them included the statement that "a portion of the temple of Atlantis may yet be discovered under the slime of ages of seawater—near what is known as Bimini, off the coast of Florida." Later, in 1940, Cayce predicted the rise of the western section of Atlantis in twenty-eight years; "and Poseidia will be among the first portions of Atlantis to rise again. Expect it in sixty-eight and sixty-nine [1968 and 1969]. Not so far away!"

The earliest discoveries in the Bimini area go back to 1956. A group of vertical marble columns was then reported in sixty feet of water. In 1958, Dr. William Bell, of Marion, North Carolina, found a six-foot column to the west of the island. It was reported by Robert Ferro and Michael Grumley in their *Atlantis; the Autobiography of a Search* (1970) as "protruding from a double circular gearlike base. . . . The photographs taken in 1958 showed peculiar emanations of light from the base of the shaft." Real excitement, however, began in 1968. A year earlier Dimitri Rebikoff, inventor and underwater archaeologist, had observed from the air a large rectangle located north of Andros. Then, during the summer of 1968, two pilots, Robert Brush and Trigg Adams, who were members of the ARE and had been looking for the evidences predicted in the Cayce readings, observed what has since been called the temple site north of Andros, and just off Pine Cay. It is a structure with the approximate dimensions of sixty by one hundred feet. The two pilots reported their discovery to Dr. J. Manson Valentine, a Miami archaeologist and zoologist, and Rebikoff. These two then went to the location and found walls three feet thick, skillfully worked in limestone, and recognized that the temple site approximates the floor plan of the so-called Temple of the Turtles in Uxmal, Yucatán. A news story dated August 23, 1968, quoted by Brad Steiger in his *Atlantis Rising* (1973), released Dr. Valentine's account of the "temple," which was located in six feet of water, the top two feet standing above the ocean floor. Within a mile of the so-called temple, Valentine and Rebikoff found two other submerged structures and since that time a total of twelve different structures have been located underwater in the Andros area.

The same year, on September 2, while looking for various reported sites off Bimini, Dr. Valentine and others found two so-called walls protruding about three feet above the sea bottom and extending for about eighteen hundred feet in a line approximately parallel to the shoreline. This was a short distance off Paradise Point, North Bimini Island. Dr. Valentine described the discovery in an article, "Archaeological Enigmas of Florida and the Western Bahamas," published by the Miami Museum of Science's *Muse News* (June 1969). In Dr. Valentine's words, he saw "an extensive pavement of rectangular and polygonal flat stones of varying size and thickness, obviously shaped and accurately aligned to form a convincingly artifactual pattern. These stones had evidently lain submerged over a long span of time, for the edges of the biggest ones had become rounded off, giving the blocks the domed appearance of giant loaves of bread or pillows. Some were absolutely rectangular, sometimes approaching perfect squares." Dr. Valentine was joined on this expedition by his sponsor, William Lord, and his son, Carter Lord. Pino Turolla, underwater explorer, was the photographer. In a later *Muse News* article, "Culture Pattern Seen" (April 1973), Dr. Valentine observed that within several months these walls were covered by sand, but not before a photographic mosaic was made by Rebikoff from his submarine, *Pegasus*.

In February 1969 Valentine and Rebikoff joined forces with a Cayce group, the Marine Archaeological Research Society (MARS). During the last week of February 1969 this group found another wall about three hundred feet long and about thirty feet wide. This expedition is described by Robert Ferro and Michael Grumley in their book *Atlantis; the Autobiography of a Search* (1970). They, Margaret Adams, Marguerite Barbrook, Dr. Lloyd Hotchkiss, and Peter Stello, were present with Dr. Valentine. According to Ferro and Grumley, later, on March 15, 1969, sponsored by Carter

56

Lord, Pino Turolla dived in fifteen to thirty-five feet of water on the Bimini Road site and noted that the rock had a metallic sound when struck. Turolla's wife, Renee, Dr. Valentine, and his wife, Ann, were also a part of this expedition.

Between July 12 and November 29 of the same year, Turolla found and photographed forty-four pillars three to five feet long and two to three feet in diameter. These were reported to be west of the Bimini Road site in fifteen feet of water. Another account of Turolla's dive, by Robert Marx (*Argosy*, November 1971), says that the pillars were from three to six feet in diameter and three to fourteen feet long, and some were standing upright. In this second account they were also described as being located in a perfect circle. A similar finding of marble columns by Turolla was reported about a mile south of the initial find.

In 1970 another survey of the features off Paradise Point off Bimini was conducted by John Gifford, graduate student, Division of Marine Geology, University of Miami, who was the chief scientist; Richard Benson, assistant professor, marine science technology, Miami-Dade Junior College; Nicholas Chitty, graduate student, Fisheries Division; Patrick Colin, graduate student, Division of Marine Biology; and Dr. John E. Hall, associate professor of archaeology, University of Miami. This group dived eighteen man-hours on December 7, 1970. In October 1971 John Gifford, assisted by Talbot Shaw Lindstrom, president of the Washington, D.C., Scientific Exploration and Archaeological Society (SEAS), made another survey. Gifford and Lindstrom returned for a further expedition April 1972. Lindstrom later described these expeditions in a paper presented at the University of Georgia's 1973 symposium, "Cultural Heritage." Gifford's October 1971 expedition had the sponsorship of the National Geographic Society and the University of Miami.

The upshot of these expeditions is the following question: Are certain features located underwater off Paradise Point, North Bimini Island, Bahamas, the work of man or nature? Are they geological or archaeological features? In *Beneath the Seas of the West Indies; Caribbean, Bahamas, Florida, Bermuda* (n.d.), Dr. Hall gave his account of the expeditions cited above. He said this: "Our investigation, sponsored by the National Geographic Society, revealed that these stones constitute a natural phenomenon called pleistocene beach-rock erosion and cracking. . . . We found no evidence whatsoever of any work of human hand or any kind of engineering,

57

and, therefore, alas for those who believe in the old legend, another Atlantis is dismissed."

On the other hand, John Gifford's report from the December field survey (dated February 25, 1971) includes these findings: (1) "It seems unlikely that the joint stress which caused the tensional jointing would not have produced such jointing in other areas." (2) "It is unlikely that tensional jointing would abruptly terminate against an unbroken block." (3) The "bedrock" beneath the blocks "showed absolutely no sign of jointing or cracking." (4) "The rock type comprising the blocks cannot be correlated with any certainty with any other rock outcropping in the area." (5) "None of the evidence . . . disproves human intervention on their formation." Later, in *The International Journal of Nautical Archaeology and Underwater Exploration* (1973), Gifford reversed himself and labeled the Bimini formation "a natural beach-rock deposit."

On the first of January 1974 we set sail from Galveston in our nine-ton sloop, *Makai II,* bound for Florida and the Bahamas. It was our intent to resolve as much of the confusion as possible and, if possible, to decide for ourselves whether this was an archaeological or geological site. Our approach was primarily a photographic reconnaissance underwater and from the air. The expedition was both a training exercise and a prospecting trip to see if further work was indicated in the area. The expedition was privately financed, and I took leave from Lamar University for a semester without pay for the occasion.

Northers in the northern gulf made the trip a fast passage of seven and one-half days. The passage to Saint Petersburg included twenty-four hours of gale-force winds and seas up to sixteen feet. In Miami two people were especially helpful. F. G. Walton Smith, retiring dean of the University of Miami's School of Marine and Atmospheric Sciences, made available to us John A. Gifford's field report of December. Dr. J. Manson Valentine, the discoverer of the Bimini Road site, also was most helpful. He spent hours with us marking out charts and showing us his slides of the area, in both underwater and aerial views.

Dr. Valentine collaborated with Charles Berlitz on two books: *Mysteries from Forgotten Worlds* (1972) and *The Bermuda Triangle* (1974). Dr. Valentine, a Yale zoologist and archaeologist, has made discoveries in the Pacific and Mexico. For the past fifteen years he has explored the Grand Bahama Banks from both the air and underwater. He has located over thirty sites on the Banks, many of which he detailed for us on our charts when we were in Miami. The most dramatic discovery he showed us was a small underwater city of perhaps four or five acres. It is on the southern extremity of the Banks, and from the air it resembles the ancient mud cities of the Peruvian coastal plains. Dr. Valentine began his aerial photographic surveys in the Bahamas in 1958.

Well briefed by Dr. Valentine, we planned to concentrate on two sites in the Bimini area: the so-called Bimini Road site just off Paradise Point; and to the east of North Bimini, a triangular-shaped underwater area that gives the impression of having possibly been an ancient reservoir. (See Figure 1)

After five weeks of diving and photography, both underwater and from the air, and taking fathometer profiles over the Bimini Road site, it became clear to us that the so-called Bimini Road is not only archaeological but worthy of further and more detailed investigation. The reasons that have led us to consider it an archaeological site are as follows: (1) The overall layout is approximately eighteen hundred feet in a very straight line. This is the standing part of a huge J whose shorter vertical member faces the beach. This latter section contains two parallel rows of stones about three hundred feet long. (2) The blocks repeat square and rectangular shapes. (3) The blocks are different thicknesses. (4) The blocks are not attached to the sea floor. (5) Composition is micrite, not the soft oolitic of the usual Bahamian beach rock. (6) According to our chart work, the layout is not exactly parallel with the beach, but is, instead, approximately seven degrees out of alignment. (Rebikoff had found the difference to be fourteen degrees.) (7) The eastern and western rows of the three-hundred-foot section (separated by about fifty yards) were recorded on our fathometer as at the same depth; *i.e.,* they were not sloping. (See Figure 2) Beach rock in the area is formed on a slope.

Upon our return to the U.S., in one of our aerial photos from the last flight we took, we found indications of an underwater structure seaward of the eighteen-hundred-foot Bimini Road site. This may correspond to Pino Turolla's find (the circular arrangement of columns).

To the east of Bimini lies a triangular-shaped area of deeper water that may be as much as several hundred acres in extent. It was earlier observed by Dr. Valentine from the air. Our aerial photographs show hydraulic action from tidal cur-

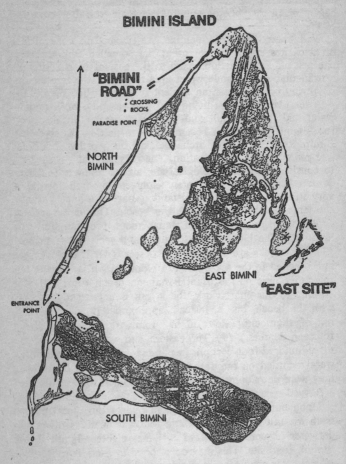

FIGURE 1

rents over this area, which reveals diversion of these currents by what appears to be a dike shape under sand. Other than the effects on current, the "dike" is evident from sea-grass patterns.

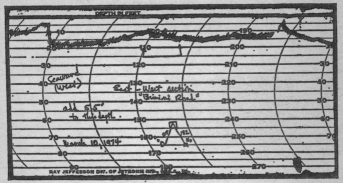

FIGURE 2

While anchored near this site, a clairvoyant aboard *Makai II* got this reading: "Atlantis lies beneath you. Only in time will its relics be discovered. However, there is something that can be done now on the east of the island. Explore the aqueduct there, close to the rim, right side" (February 11, 1974). Later I personally received a clairvoyant impression of a stone-cased well head twelve feet in diameter at the east of the "dike." Still later, back in Miami, Dr. Valentine told us that the psychic Irene Hughes had described the site to him as a reservoir. Dr. Valentine had probed five feet under the grass patterns of the dike before our visit.

In June 1974 at Virginia Beach, during a visit with Hugh Lynn, Edgar Evans, and Gail Cayce, we saw a photograph of a well found much earlier on the east shore of North Bimini.

While still at the site of North Bimini, we utilized a small floating air compressor to operate an airlift. With it we probed nine feet down through the sand. This was in very shallow water, and therefore the airlift was slow and inefficient. Our probe was through one of the sea-grass patterns of the "dike." We found no underlying stone at that depth. We have since devised a more simple method of probing at least thirty feet. When we return, we intend to probe for a possible stone structure that seems to be influencing and patterning the growth of the sea grass.

The sites we have focused upon promise ultimately to have great significance. We are, however, still at the stage where more evidence must be gathered to convince the archaeological world that Bimini does in fact possess what are truly the remnants of an ancient culture. From the scientific point of view, at this point it would be senseless to attempt to identify the culture. Those who have seen our slides of the Bimini area, however, recognize that the sites are not accidents of nature.

II

PIECES
OF
THE RIDDLE

The Vanished USS *Cyclops:*
Three Appraisals

President Woodrow Wilson, commenting on the disappearance of the USS Cyclops, said, "Only God and the sea know what happened to the great ship." The U.S. Navy observed that it was "one of the most baffling mysteries" in its annals, as all attempts to find the vessel had "proved unsuccessful" and that no one theory "satisfactorily accounts for her disappearance."

The Cyclops mystery occurred during World War I, and the Navy was unable to undertake an immediate and thorough investigation. As a result, it remains one of the most striking examples of unsolved nautical disasters in the Bermuda Triangle area. Three separate appraisals of the Cyclops case, presented on the following pages, throw light on the mystery from different directions, enabling the reader to gain an objective view of this unique event in twentieth-century naval history.

7. The *Cyclops* Mystery

by Conrad A. Nervig

Over and over again, accounts dealing with the Bermuda Triangle mysteries speak of the disappearance of the USS Cyclops, in the midst of World War I. The case has been reviewed and analyzed so extensively that in many of the published accounts it has taken on the character of a legend. Mr. Nervig, however, whose own account originally appeared in the U.S. Naval Institute Proceedings, speaks from personal experience and background that defies legend-making and the temptations to a modern mythology. Although this account speaks of the ship as having last been seen in the port of Bahia, Brazil, others state that it was observed later in Barbados.

On 21 February 1918, the USS *Cyclops* steamed into the harbor of Bahia, Brazil, took aboard mail from the naval vessels at anchor there and at 6:00 P.M. departed, bound for Baltimore, Maryland. This was the last ever seen of the *Cyclops*. She never arrived at her destination nor was any trace of her ever reported, thereby adding her name to the unsolved mysteries of the sea.

In the capacity of watch officer, I served on board this vessel on the voyage that took her from her homeport of Norfolk, Virginia, to Rio de Janeiro, at which port I was detached and ordered to the USS *Glacier*. The *Cyclops* disappeared on the voyage returning to the United States.

Throughout the years that have elapsed since that event, many theories have been advanced as to the probable cause of the catastrophe, though none, in my opinion, even slightly approaches a solution of the mystery.

In writing this, I am motivated by a desire to set down various facts and incidents as I saw them in the hope that some light may be thrown on the subject. While some of these may appear to be somewhat inconsequential, they may have had some bearing on the disappearance of the *Cyclops*. For the compiling of this record, I have had to rely solely on memory and the few terse entries in a diary containing little except dates, ports, and ship movements. The day-to-day story of events was more fully covered in letters to my wife, which were in the mail on board the *Cyclops* when she went down.

The USS *Cyclops* was a twin-screw, naval auxiliary vessel of the latest type, designed and built by the Navy for service as a Fleet collier. She was commanded by Lieutenant Commander George W. Worley, U.S. Naval Reserve Force.

Commander Worley was a gruff, eccentric salt of the old school, given to carrying a cane, but possessing few other cultural attainments. He was a very indifferent seaman and a poor, overly cautious navigator. Unfriendly and taciturn, he was generally disliked by both his officers and men.

Prior to the entry of the United States into World War I, Captain Worley was a member of the U.S. Naval Auxiliary Service. In this hybrid organization, the ships were operated for the Navy and took orders from the Bureau of Operations. This service comprised the colliers, cargo, refrigerator, and hospital ships and was, as the name implies, auxiliary to the fleet. The personnel was civilian under the jurisdiction of the Navy Department. In 1917, shortly after the declaration of war, the ships of the Auxiliary Service were taken into the Navy, the officers being enrolled in the U.S. Naval Reserve Force.

The *Cyclops* departed from the Navy Yard, Norfolk, Virginia, on 8 January 1918, loaded down to her Plimsoll mark with a cargo of coal, mail, and miscellaneous stores destined for the South American Patrol Fleet, then operating on the east coast of South America. The day had dawned overcast and cold, with a light snow falling. For days the harbor had been completely frozen over. Liberty parties from ships at anchor walked on the ice that morning returning to their ships. In plowing through the ice floes in the ship channel, the *Cyclops* narrowly averted a collision with the USS *Survey*, outward bound to the Mediterranean for patrol and antisubmarine duty. This was the first of the untoward incidents that dogged her on that final voyage. By nightfall, she had cleared the Virginia Capes and headed southward, breasting the heavy winter seas with a speed and ease amazing for such a heavily loaded vessel.

About 8:00 P.M., as I groped my way forward on the darkened deck to relieve the officer of the watch, I was mystified at hearing a sound not unlike that caused by metal

66

plates being rubbed together. Upon investigation, I found this to be the case. The ship was working to the extent that where steam or water pipes passed through web irons, or were in contact with portions of the hull, the movement could be distinctly seen. Later, in daylight, by sighting fore or aft along the well deck, the movement was very perceptible; the deck amidships rising and falling as if the ship were conforming to the contour of the seas. Later that day when I called it to the Captain's attention, he shrugged it off with a superior, "Son, she'll last as long as we do"—which was, indeed, partly true.

On the fifth day out, the Captain ordered Lieutenant Forbes, the executive officer, to his room under arrest following a trivial disagreement about ship's work. From all reports, this seemed to be a routine matter in ships commanded by Captain Worley.

In the evening of this same day, Ensign Cain, one of the watch and division officers, apparently in good health, was placed on the sick list and ordered to bed by the doctor. It was the general opinion in the wardroom that this was done to save Mr. Cain from being a victim of the Commanding Officer's unreasoning temper. I do not recall that the doctor made any comment nor that he was in any way questioned regarding the matter; his act and motive were taken for granted.

At this time Mr. Cain's watch duty had been the midwatch and it fell my lot to relieve him. I do not remember being at all unhappy with the assignment. The balmy, tropical nights under a full moon were a pleasant escape from the gloomy atmosphere of the wardroom. During this period of duty, I became very well acquainted with Commander Worley.

Directly below the navigation bridge, on the starboard side, was a small cabin which the Captain occupied when at sea. Shortly after taking over the watch at midnight, I was somewhat startled to see him coming up the starboard ladder dressed in long woolen underwear, a derby hat, and a cane. I frantically searched my memory for something I had done wrong or had neglected to do. He neither apologized for his attire, nor even so much as mentioned it, and my salute and "Good morning, Captain," could not have been more correct or military. His affability soon relieved my anxiety, as I realized this was no official call, but a purely social one.

This visit lasted some two hours, and as we leaned against the forward bridge rail, he regaled me with stories of his home and numerous incidents of his long life at sea. He had a fund of tales, mostly humorous. These nocturnal visits became a regular routine, and I rather enjoyed them. His uniform, if it could be so called, never varied from what he had worn on that first occasion. I have often wondered to what I owed these visits—his fondness for me or his sleeplessness. That he liked me, I was sure, for when in Rio de Janeiro I received orders detaching me from the *Cyclops*, he sought to have those orders revoked. Fortunately, for me, he was unsuccessful.

On the twelfth day, we came in sight of the coast of South America off Pernambuco, at a distance of about twenty miles. The Captain immediately changed course to take us farther out. We came to anchor off the city of Bahia on 22 January 1918, after running forty-eight miles past the entrance to the harbor. Three more hours of darkness, steaming on that course, would have had her aground. The navigator had protested, pointing out the error of these decisions, but had been brusquely overruled.

While in this port, we supplied coal and stores to that venerable veteran of Manila Bay, the USS *Raleigh*. The *Cyclops*, upon getting underway from alongside, twice fouled her, fortunately with only slight damage.

On the voyage south to Rio de Janeiro, the head of the starboard engine high pressure cylinder blew off. The remainder of the trip was made running on one engine. At Rio, the balance of the cargo was distributed to the various vessels of the South American Patrol Fleet at anchor there. I was detached and ordered to the USS *Glacier*, greatly relieved that my tour of duty in the *Cyclops* had finally terminated without any unpleasant personal incidents.

For her return voyage, the *Cyclops* proceeded to take aboard a cargo of manganese ore. It was during this period that her most tragic accident up to that time occurred. One of the ship's boats, a motor sailer with a seaman on board, had been tied up to the quarter boom, when without warning one of the engines was turned over, resulting in the boat being drawn into the propeller. The man was injured, knocked overboard, and drowned. This negligence, I feel, can be laid squarely at the feet of the Commanding Officer, who by his irrational methods of command had so thoroughly demoralized and disorganized the officers and men of the *Cyclops*.

On 15 February, the *Glacier* got underway and proceeded

out of the harbor with a Brazilian pilot boat leading the way through the mine fields guarding the entrance.

Excerpt from my diary:

> February 21, 1918, Bahia, Brazil. USS *Cyclops* stood in *from the North*. Took mail aboard and departed at 6:00 P.M. for Baltimore.

As Bahia lies north of Rio de Janeiro, the *Cyclops* should have been seen coming from the south. Again the familiar example of navigation as practiced on board that vessel.

During her short stay in Bahia, the *Cyclops'* paymaster, Carrol G. Page, my best friend, came aboard the *Glacier* on official business. (He was a grandson of Senator Page, Chairman of the Senate Naval Committee.) At his departure, I, as officer of the deck, escorted him to the gangway. On leaving, he grasped my hand in both of his and said very solemnly, "Well, goodbye, old man, and God bless you." I was deeply impressed with his finality, which was truly prophetic in its implication.

When the *Cyclops* steamed out that evening, she was taking her last departure. She was never seen again.

There have been many theories put forth as to the cause of the disaster that overtook the *Cyclops*. I will enumerate some of the ones previously written up as most likely; also, the one I am firmly convinced was the real one.

(1) *Storms*. This can be discounted, as there were no storms of any great intensity recorded during the period of her disappearance.

(2) *She was torpedoed*. This we can also discount, as it is highly improbable the entire crew would have perished. The coast was not so distant it could not have been safely navigated in a ship's boat. During the submarine sinkings in the Atlantic, wreckage from sunken vessels was quite common. Not one scrap identified as being from the *Cyclops* has ever been found. During convoy service, I saw two abandoned life boats from different vessels plainly marked with their ship's names. In view of this, I am firmly convinced that the *Cyclops* went down with all her boats in their cradles, or at their davits, firmly secured for sea. Furthermore, the German authorities after the war had ended declared that none of their submarines had been in that area during the period in question.

(3) *Her cargo shifted; she rolled on her beam ends, and*

then filled and sank. This I consider highly improbable, as manganese ore by reason of its weight and shape would shift very little, if at all.

(4) *She broke in two.* This, in view of the known evidence, I am forced to accept.

It will be recalled that the *Cyclops* loaded a cargo of manganese ore; we have no knowledge of the manner in which that cargo was stowed. The only other officer with experience in cargo-handling, the executive officer, was confined to his room under arrest, so it is quite probable the task of supervising the loading was assigned to some young, inexperienced officer.

With the weight of manganese ore, and its lack of bulk, the holds would be only partially filled when the vessel was down to her load line. Now, if this weight was confined to only two or three holds, and those holds in the amidship section, the vessel's inherent weakness would be greatly accentuated. Properly stowed, this cargo would be distributed in several holds throughout most of the length of the ship.

Assuming that the vessel under stress at sea broke in two, probably in the region just forward of the engine and boiler room spaces, the inrushing water and weight of the cargo would cause the two sections, as they sank lower in the water, to assume a vertical position. Then, as the holds filled, they would go down carrying all evidence with them. This would have happened in the course of a very few minutes and would account for the fact that no SOS call was heard nor, so far as we know, were there any lifeboats launched from the ill-fated ship.

As I recall, the deck of the *Cyclops* had few articles that would float and support a man. It is questionable that any of the crew surviving the sinking was able to reach one of these; it would only have served to prolong his life, not to save it.

Of all the officers and men who lost their lives in that disaster, only three can be said to have had little to lose: three General Courts Martial prisoners convicted of the horrible murder of a shipmate and sentenced to prison terms ranging from fifty to ninety-nine years. These men undoubtedly died, locked in their cells, when the ship sank with all her secrets.

8. Did the *Cyclops* Turn Turtle?

by Mahlon S. Tisdale

The preceding contribution to this anthology, summarizing "The Cyclops Mystery," analyzed the curious disappearance of this vessel from the point of view of a close personal observer. The following account, by Lieutenant Commander Tisdale, is a daring analysis of the conditions, hazards, and possibilities for disaster that were unique to the Cyclops case. This account originally appeared in the U.S. Naval Institute Proceedings in 1920, shortly after the Cyclops' disappearance, and it therefore has an immediacy and closeness to the subject that cannot be equaled by narratives written at a later date.

ALTHOUGH the loss of the USS *Cyclops* bids fair to be one of the mysteries of the war, many theories have been advanced during the usual "ward room arguments," the general consensus of opinion being that she capsized. This deduction is always made, it seems to me, because, although the finale of the conversation is to the effect that "surely something would have floated," no other solution seems at all tenable. In other words, a good many officers agree that she capsized, but few have any good reason to offer as proof of this belief.

Through a peculiar train of circumstances I happened to live through an incident which I believe lends a certain plausibility to the capsizing theory.

In December, 1914, I was ordered to the USS *Neptune* as a part of her commissioning complement. During the first few months after going into commission considerable trouble was experienced in keeping the ship on an even keel—even when alongside the dock. She was built with athwartship double bottoms fitted with baffles but in such a way as to permit water to move completely across the ship during a list or a roll. Running along the side of the ship immediately under the main deck were "topside tanks." These tanks extended outboard from the coaling hatches to the outer skin in an athwartship direction, had a sloping bottom which extended down some eight feet (estimated), and the series of tanks ran from the forward bridge to the break of the poop on each side of the ship. In the weather deck, on each side of the ship, was fitted a series of manhole plates each giving access to one topside tank. These were not manhole plates in the usual meaning of the term, but resembled the circular brass bunker plates as used on battleships. The bottom of the *Neptune* was flat and the double bottoms ran all the way across the flat. The topside tanks, as can be seen from the above description, were high above the keel and extended only some one-third of the distance from the sheer strake to the center line. A considerable purchase could thus be obtained by filling topside tanks; and a slight list caused by an excess of water in the tanks of one side would soon increase considerably, due to the free water in the double bottoms, which would, of course, immediately rush across the ship. This is assuming that the bottoms were not full.

As the *Cyclops* was similar in construction to the *Neptune* it is fair to assume that conditions of trim obtaining on one obtained also on the other. I have seen the *Neptune* "flop" ten degrees for no apparent reason. If in so flopping something suddenly occurred to accentuate the list, such as the flooding of the topside tanks on the down side, is it not perfectly plausible to assume that this accentuation might have increased to such a degree as to cause the ship to turn turtle?

The *Neptune* was of some 19,600 tons displacement when loaded to capacity with 10,500 tons of coal. The ratio between cargo and total displacement gives an idea of the great freeboard existing when the ship was entirely empty. This freeboard was so considerable that although the motion of the ship in a seaway was more than noticeable it was unusual to take water over the main deck abaft the break of the forecastle when the ship was light.

This was exemplified by my experience on the *Cyclops*.

In the fall of 1916, while attached to the USS *Pennsylvania*, I was detailed to make a ten-day trip on the *Cyclops* as communication officer for the war game, held that year. We got underway at Newport and followed our flagship—the *Vestal*—together with two or three other colliers representing the "black" fleet or the "red" fleet—I am a little hazy on the particular shade of the rainbow involved in this battle—toward the rendezvous from which we were to begin our attack on the United States. Each of our "fleet" was towing a destroyer in order to save its fuel until the opening day of the fight.

On the afternoon of the second day it began to blow. One by one the towlines parted. Captain Worley (Master USNAS) of the *Cyclops,* gave our tow—the *Conyngham*—all the line we had available and by so doing and by the *Conyngham* going ahead slow to ease the strain, we managed to hold our tow until all the other colliers had parted lines; but eventually ours snapped and as the sea was then too rough to attempt picking up another line the destroyers were forced to come ahead on their own. The *Vestal* alone succeeded in holding her tow, and I believe that she had a towing engine.

The *Cyclops* had only one thousand tons of coal distributed among her various cargo holds and was riding high out of the water. The wind had worked itself into a gale and had beaten up a very rough sea. The destroyers were rolling so that it did not appear physically possible for them all to come through safely. During the afternoon of the third day conditions had grown steadily worse. The captain asked me to remain on the bridge while he went aft for supper. Upon his return—this was the evening of the third day out—I fought my way aft, wrapped myself around the particular stanchion that I had come to regard as mine, hurriedly ate a sandwich or two, filled my pockets with oranges for the long night ahead of me and started back to the bridge.

On each side of these colliers, inboard against the cargo hatches, run the steam lines for the winches and for the auxiliary machinery forward. These pipes are encased with light sheet metal and the cover is corrugated as are fire room floorplates. This forms a runway leading from the break of the forecastle aft to the break of the poop. The men call this the "bicycle track" for no better reason I suppose than that one could not ride a bicycle on it.

In going back to the bridge from the wardroom I started along the bicycle track as usual, but as I came abreast the manhole plate for the starboard after topside tank I was thrown off the track onto the main deck. We had lifelines rigged to assist in walking forward and aft, but the lurch of the ship broke my hold. I landed near the topside tank manhole and my attention was at once caught by the fact that the plate was *not secured.* I slid the plate into position as best I could with one hand—I was carrying a sigcode book—and set up the central screw finger-tight, thinking all the time I worked how fortunate it was that I had served on the *Neptune* and had there learned the value of keeping tank tops tight. On starting forward again I was astonished to find that the next plate was also cast off. Upon looking further, all plates were seen to be adrift. Deciding that securing all of them was too much of a job to do with one hand, I fought my way to the bridge and reported to the captain that someone had opened all of the topside tanks. He laughed at my earnestness and said that they were *always left off* in accordance with instructions from the navy yard (I won't mention the yard, as I never saw the circular during my time in the colliers), as the air was "better for the bitumastic." The skipper was worrying not at all about the tanks. We were cavorting around the old ocean like a frisky colt, but, true enough, were taking no green seas over the main deck. As I have said, we were light and high out of the water. The captain was worrying about his cargo. With such a small amount of coal in the cargo holds and with no braces rigged to hold it in place, it was not improbable that the cargo might shift.

Standing at the clinometer that night I saw it register 48 degrees to port and 56 to starboard. (Now you destroyer men consider the size of the ship before you compare notes disparagingly.) So much for proof that these ships can roll when tempted. During this rolling she was dry so far as green seas were concerned, but this was due to her freeboard. I have seen the *Neptune* at full load ship seas on her well deck which carried away the side plating on the bicycle track to such an extent that we had to heave to for repairs.

Now let us take the case of the *Cyclops* on her ill-fated voyage of last year when she was lost. She was carrying manganese ore (according to newspaper reports we received abroad at the time). Due to the great weight per cubic foot of this ore as compared to coal it is probable that her cargo holds were loaded by weight and not by volume and were therefore far from full. Perhaps the cargo was braced to prevent shifting—but this would have required very strong braces, far beyond the capacity of the ship's carpenter. Unless these braces were installed at the loading port they were probably not installed at all. Now the matter sizes up as follows:

The ship was heavily loaded—hence deep in the water with a correspondingly small freeboard—but her holds were not full by *volume*.

It was customary to leave the manhole plates off the topside tanks according to the statement of the captain (she had the same captain when I made my cruise on her as she had when she was lost) in order to "preserve the bitumastic."

Due to her load her sea connections from the topside tanks

were probably submerged. These were in the skin of the ship and led from the bottom of the tank.

In any sort of storm it was always customary in the colliers, due to their liveliness and to their great amount of top hamper, to secure *everything* for sea. I have seen even the huge iron sister-blocks, which are shackled to the fore and aft girder, lashed together to prevent pounding.

Is it not plausible to assume that the cargo may have shifted, perhaps only a little, but enough to increase the average list sufficiently to cause the free water in the double bottoms to rush toward the down side thus further increasing the list? Suppose the heavily laden *Cyclops* now shipped a sea. Would not this sea run into the open manholes of the topside tanks and immediately give the ship a tendency to capsize?

This could all occur in a few seconds and the ship would be bottom up before anyone could abandon ship. Some few men from the bridge and poop might have been thrown clear of the ship. But with everything secured for sea there would be little wreckage. Remember that there would be nothing adrift except such gear as would be free to float off during the few seconds during the turn. There would be no debris such as always follows a sinking due to other marine casualty, as in the case of striking a mine or torpedo. There would have been no time for an SOS. There would have been no time for anything. The few men in the water could not have lived long of their own accord. Such small gear as did float off would have been lost in the vastness of the ocean long before the rescue vessels started their search.

This seems to me a plausible solution of the loss of the *Cyclops*. Of course it is only a theory based upon several assumptions, some of which may be faulty. As several officers have said, "Yours seems to be the only plausible theory." it occurred to me that the service as a whole might be interested.

9. Before the *Cyclops*

from The Literary Digest

The two preceding contributions have dealt with the disappearance of the USS Cyclops *from supplementary points of view. But how did Americans, at the time of the ship's disappearance, hear of it, and in what perspective was it viewed at the time? From the pages of the now defunct but once widely read* Literary Digest *(June 8, 1918) comes an account that speaks of the* Cyclops *in terms of previous disappearances of a similarly mysterious nature—proving, among other things, that bafflement over the disappearance of naval vessels is not just a current fad, but dates back for at least a half-century.*

SHALL the *Cyclops* be added to the list of vessels that have "arrived" at the Port of Missing Ships? Each day the mystery of her fate deepens. Modern, stanch, well-manned and equipped, to those who are familiar with the sea and navigation the disappearance of the collier is inexplicable. If the *Cyclops* must be added to the "Missing" she will be the first ship with a wireless equipment to enter that port.

Some wreckage floated ashore to tell the fate of the German cruiser *Karlsruhe,* but no such messenger had arrived from the *Cyclops.* The New York *Evening Sun* says:

"Many instances point to the probability that the misfortune of the *Cyclops* may never be known. Other vessels, well built to withstand all the treacheries of the seas, have succumbed. One such vessel was the *Naronic.* She was a large freight-vessel, the first of the twin-screw type to be built for the cargo trade. She was made of steel and had eight bulkheads to prevent sinking.

"Just what happened to the *Naronic* has never been discovered. She steamed from Liverpool. Days passed and then cables began to hum as both sides of the ocean queried about her delay. Finally, some weeks later, a capsized life-boat was

76

found with the word *Naronic* on her stern. That was all. How, when, or where she entered the Port of Missing Ships is not known, but it is there she rests. She was equipped to resist storms and had been called the 'biggest, safest, swiftest sea-carrier' of her times, but the sea included her in its toll.

"In recent years few passenger-vessels have disappeared. In the days of sail and side-wheelers, however, a number of large vessels loaded with passengers were swallowed up, perhaps the victims of an uncharted rock, a heavy gale, a tidal wave, or a fire. One of these was the *City of Glasgow*. In 1854 she sailed from England with 480 passengers, most of them emigrants bound for Castle Garden. No trace of her was ever found.

"Two years later the *Pacific* of the Collins line sailed from New York for Europe with 186 passengers. For months following her disappearance other vessels sought for her in vain. In those days the ocean lanes had not been adopted and there was no means of knowing where best to search.

"Other vessels have disappeared, but have left very definite impressions of what happened to them. One such was the *President*, which is generally believed to have foundered in a gale off the New England coast. Another vessel, the *Coventry*, saw her in the midst of the storm, making heavy weather of it.

"The *President* left New York on March 11, 1841. Among her passengers was Tyrone Power, the Irish actor. She was in command of Captain Roberts. Two months later a bottle was washed up on the shore of Cape Cod with the cryptic message, '*President* sunk in storm.'

"In 1870 the *City of Boston*, with two hundred passengers, left Liverpool never to return. It was believed that she was the victim of a severe storm which came up a few days after she left port. Bits of wreckage were seen at sea some months later with her name on them. Such an impression also prevails regarding the sinking of the *Portland*, which left Boston Harbor for Portland in the fall of 1898. There was a severe blizzard that night, and it is generally thought an extra heavy sea caught her under the paddle-wheel and overturned her.

"On August 28, 1883, the *Inchclutha* left Calcutta for Hull with a cargo of wheat. The following day the *Cherubini* left Sunderland for Genoa with a cargo of coal. Neither of these vessels was ever reported again. On March 9, 1885, the *Magneta* was seen passing out of the English Channel bound for Singapore with a load of cable. She also carried nine passengers. She was never sighted again."

Sometimes a vessel is found abandoned at sea without any explanation, or means of discovering the cause of her condition. Such a case was that of the *Yula Maru,* a Japanese steamship found in mid-ocean with eight dead men on her deck. What had become of the rest of the crew was never known. The greatest mystery is that of the *Marie Celeste.* Says *The Sun:*

"She was discovered with all sails set headed toward Gibraltar. There was no sign of life aboard the vessel nor, most unusual of all, was there any sign of her having been abandoned. Everything was in order, boats were all in place and ropes were neatly coiled.

"The only thing missing, as nearly as could be found, was the ship's chronometer. However, the captain's watch was found in his cabin. There was nothing in the log to tell a tale of storm, disease, fire, or other disaster.

"Many surmises have been made regarding the mystery, and books have even been written suggesting a solution. One of these insists that the passengers must all have gone in swimming except the captain. He, it says, must have been timing a race with the chronometer, his watch being broken, when the vessel gave a lurch, threw him overboard and sailed away before any of the swimmers could reach her.

"Another surmise, made seriously by its author, is that all hands were standing by the rail when a tidal wave spilled them off. This theory has been generally laughed at, it being pointed out that such a thing would not have been possible without deranging the equipment on the decks. All this was years ago, and it is almost certain that her mystery will never be solved.

"Had it not been for the wireless it is doubtful whether the world would ever have known the circumstances of the *Titanic's* sinking. Undoubtedly many other vessels before the days of wireless and ocean lanes entered the Port of Missing Ships through the ice.

"The Hun fang-reef of *'spurlos versenkt'* has of course added another hazard to the many of the sea, and it is just possible that the *Cyclops* may have gone in this way. However, that is merely conjecture, and even those who support it believe it unlikely that she would have been sunk without having sent word by wireless."

The *Cyclops* was loaded with manganese, which is much needed by the nations at war. The vessel was commanded by Lieutenant-Commander George W. Worley, who was born in

Germany, his name being George Wichman. He came to this country as a child, was adopted by a man named Worley in California, and when he grew up applied to the court to change his name, taking that of the man who had befriended him. He became an American citizen in 1893. The New York *World* says:

"Before Captain Worley sailed on his last voyage on the *Cyclops* he disposed of some property he owned in Norfolk, Virginia, including the home his wife and child live in. He told friends that when he returned from the voyage he intended to get an extended leave of absence and go back to California and rest. He said he had to have an operation performed and it would take about six months for him to recover his strength.

"Mrs. Worley says her husband is a good American and that his long and faithful record in the Government service proves it. She says she believes he is still alive, that his vessel is probably disabled at sea and that he is waiting to be picked up.

" 'Do you think my husband would prove a traitor to America, to his wife and little daughter?' she asked when a reporter called on her. 'My husband was an American through and through. He hated Germany. He came here seeking freedom and he would fight and die to maintain that freedom. He is just as good an American as any man born in America, and a whole lot better than many of those who question his patriotism now. I hope he lives to settle with his traducers.' "

10. The *Atalanta* Has Vanished

by Michael Cusack

HMS Atalanta *vanished on her training voyage. Her disappearance furnishes one of the classic cases of the Bermuda Triangle mystery. The author, associate editor of* Science World, *has dealt with this subject in the magazine in an article, "The Deadly Mystery of the 'Devil's Triangle.' " He is a consultant on scientific and technology matters for Scholastic*

Magazines, has previously worked as an electronics techni-
cian in the United States Air Force (1950–1954), and has
held several positions with General Precisions, Inc. He con-
tributes regularly to the Funk & Wagnalls Encyclopedias.

CAPTAIN Francis Stirling of the Royal Navy was a cautious
man. And this sense of caution may have prompted the fateful decision that he made on January 29, 1880. While at anchor in Hamilton Harbor, Bermuda, Captain Stirling decided
to shorten the voyage of the training frigate HMS *Atalanta*.
Scrapping plans to cruise into the Caribbean Sea, the captain
charted a course from Bermuda direct to England.

Evidently Captain Stirling did not inform the Admiralty in
London of his change in plans. But he did tell his wife.

In a letter dispatched aboard a "fast" steamship on January 30, Captain Stirling wrote that he expected to reach
Spithead during the first week of March. Another letter
aboard the same steamship confirmed this expectation. Lieutenant W. H. Stephens, navigator of the *Atalanta*, wrote to a
fellow officer in Portsmouth saying that he expected to be in
England about March 1.

Neither officer gave a reason for the *Atalanta*'s planned
early return to England. The training ship was originally due
home April 4. Perhaps the misfortunes of the *Atalanta*'s outward passage gave Captain Stirling reason enough to plan a
swift voyage home.

HMS *Atalanta*'s outward passage had a clouded start. On a
grim, gray November day in 1879, fifteen officers, sixty-five
crewmen, and about two hundred midshipmen crowded
aboard the old wooden ship. Relatives of the midshipmen
lined Portsmouth docks to wish them "Godspeed." The turn-
out of relatives was unusually large. Tears and other signs
of concern were generously evident among the crowd. There
were reasons for this concern. A little over a year earlier, the
training frigate HMS *Eurydice* had foundered and taken
three hundred men and boys to watery graves. HMS
Atalanta was HMS *Eurydice*'s replacement!

Clearing Portsmouth harbor under full sail on November
7, 1879, HMS *Atalanta* was a symbol and a relic of a bygone
age. The ship was commissioned as a twenty-four-gun
frigate-of-war, HMS *Juno*, in 1845. HMS *Juno* was a ship
that Nelson could have been proud of. But it was born into a
time of change. Iron and steam were rapidly replacing wood
and canvas among fighting ships. By 1865, HMS *Juno* was
hopelessly obsolete. The once-proud ship was decommis-

sioned, renamed *Atalanta*, and anchored in Portsmouth harbor as a prison hulk.

That's how the ship might have ended its days. But the tragic loss of HMS *Eurydice* gave the old *Atalanta* a new lease on life. The Royal Navy needed a new training ship. And since the lords of the Admiralty considered that good seamanship could be learned only aboard a full-rigged sailing ship, the board of commissioners looked around for a suitable frigate. Their search took them to the prison hulk in Portsmouth harbor. The old ship's timbers were sound. So, in 1879 HMS *Atalanta* was recommissioned to replace the lost *Eurydice*. And a man renowned as a cautious navigator was picked to command the training ship.

On assuming command of HMS *Atalanta*, Captain Stirling recommended certain alterations in the old ship. Without guns, the frigate tended to be top-heavy. The captain requested that the masts be shortened, the rigging be lightened, and the ballast be increased. It's doubtful that all of these alterations were accomplished before the *Atalanta* sailed on its long voyage on November 7, 1879.

The *Atalanta* sailed southwestward to the Azores and then westward to Barbados. Along the way, the ship encountered rough weather. One crewman was lost overboard. And there was talk of trouble among the crew. Though it was never officially confirmed, Captain Stirling is said to have clapped two men in irons for refusing to go aloft. As the *Atalanta* approached Barbados, dreaded yellow fever broke out. Three men were put ashore to a Barbados hospital. And the *Atalanta* sailed north to Bermuda. There, beset by threats of epidemic, mutiny, and stormy weather, Captain Stirling seems to have decided to head straight for England.

On January 31, 1880, HMS *Atalanta* sailed out of Hamilton Harbor . . . and was never seen again.

When HMS *Atalanta* didn't show up during March, there was no hue and cry. Only Captain Stirling's wife and Lieutenant Stephens' friend expected the ship in March. And they knew enough of the changeable ways of the sea and of seafarers to anticipate other changes in *Atalanta*'s schedule. At the end of the first week in April, Admiralty officials were not concerned by *Atalanta*'s nonappearance. Sailing ships were unpredictable. Being a week late was not unusual. However, during the second week of April, the Admiralty was besieged by letters and telegrams from anxious parents. On April 13 a Navy spokesman suggested that the training ship might have been disabled or dismasted by a storm. In that case, the spokesman added, the *Atalanta* could be several weeks late.

The Admiralty was prepared to wait and see. But the relatives of the midshipmen were not prepared to wait. On April 17, two hundred of them stormed down to Whitehall and demanded action. The Admiralty responded by sending the stores ship *Wye* to the Azores to check on the whereabouts of *Atalanta*.

In the meantime, the gunboat *Avon* arrived from China. The captain of the *Avon* stepped ashore at Portsmouth on April 19, and he reported seeing wreckage all around the harbor of Fayal in the Azores. Though none of that wreckage was identified as being part of the *Atalanta*, many people in England jumped to the conclusion that the *Atalanta* had been lost off the Azores in a fierce storm that swept through the area in early April.

Then, a discovery in the sea near the Azores added a dimension to the mystery. The crew of the *Wye* found an old man adrift in a rowboat. The man was in bad shape. He died aboard the *Wye* without saying a word. The crew of a passing ship heard of the discovery. Soon all England was stirred by the rumor that a survivor of the *Atalanta* had been found. The rumor ended with the return of the *Wye*. Though the man in the boat was never identified, he was obviously older than any crew member of the *Atalanta*. Furthermore, his clothes and general appearance suggested that he was a Portuguese fisherman. The crew of the *Wye* found absolutely no trace of the *Atalanta*. The captain of the stores ship expressed doubts that the *Atalanta* had ever reached the vicinity of the Azores.

During May 1880, criticism of the Admiralty and Navy brass mounted in Britain's popular press. Writers unfavorably compared the *Atalanta* to the ill-fated *Eurydice*. "Why," they clamored, "should innocent boys be sent to sea in unstable ships?" For the first time in centuries, the Royal Navy was on the defensive. In a letter to *The Times,* Admiral Sir B. J. Sullivan objected to the comparison of the *Atalanta* to the *Eurydice.* He pointed out that the *Atalanta* belonged to a class of broad-beamed frigates that were considered by expert naval opinion to be "very safe vessels." Admiral Sullivan concluded that "... in choosing a ship of that class as a training ship, the Admiralty could not have made a safer choice."

Despite the admiral's assurances, the criticism continued. And a new development added fuel to the fire. Three seamen with yellow fever had been put ashore by the *Atalanta* at Barbados. John Verling, one of the three, survived and returned to England in late May 1880. Reporters flocked to see the survivor. And he did not disappoint them. Able-bodied seaman Verling called the *Atalanta* a "crank ship."

"She was top-heavy with a snap roll," he said. Mr. Verling also stated that some of the ship's officers were afraid that the *Atalanta* would "turn turtle."

The penny press was gleeful. But the lords of the Admiralty were definitely not amused. A high-ranking officer visited Mr. Verling in the Portsmouth Naval Hospital. And from that day on, the seaman didn't have another word to say about the lost *Atalanta*.

Even before the Verling incident, public criticism stung the Admiralty into unprecedented action. On May 5, 1880, the entire Channel Squadron of the Royal Navy was sent "to comb the sea" for the *Atalanta*. Moving in a line, the steam frigates *Minotaur, Agincourt, Achilles,* and *Northumberland* and the dispatch vessel *Salamis* swept across the eastern Atlantic Ocean from Bantry Bay to the Azores ... and back again. They found no trace of the missing training ship.

Some people at the time questioned the advisability of limiting the search for the missing *Atalanta* to the eastern section of the Atlantic. By early May 1880 it was generally known that Captain Stirling had planned to sail directly to England. In that case, the *Atalanta* should have passed north of the Azores sometime in late February or early March. So, the critics wondered, what might the *Atalanta* be doing near the Azores in April?

It seems that Admiralty officials wished to think that the *Atalanta* could have been lost only in a violent storm. And such a storm had lashed the area around the Azores in April. Furthermore, Captain Stirling's original sailing schedule would have put the *Atalanta* between the Azores and England in early April. And since they were not officially informed of any changes in this schedule, the Admiralty officials chose to follow that schedule in directing search operations.

During the months following the total disappearance of the *Atalanta*, British newspapers were filled with reports and rumors concerning the loss of the vessel. Another sailing ship—the iron-hulled merchant vessel *Bay of Biscay*—disappeared around the same time. And it was speculated that the two missing ships might have collided. The *Bay of Biscay* left Rangoon, bound for Liverpool, sometime in October 1879. The ship was last sighted off the Azores on February 7, 1880.

Could the *Atalanta* have collided with the *Bay of Biscay*? If so, where and when? What quirk of fate could have joined the different paths of these two ships? If they collided, isn't it likely that their wreckage would have been sighted? Was their wreckage sighted?

On June 14, 1880, the bark *Exile* arrived in New York from Antwerp. According to *The New York Times*, the *Exile*'s captain said that in mid-May he had passed "a large boat, bottoms up, covered with barnacles, drifting four hundred miles west of Cape Finistere [Spain]." A short time later, the captain said, he saw deck beams in the water.

Some British papers reported that here at last was evidence of the lost *Atalanta*. However, the captain's description of the boat in the water did not match the Royal Navy's description of the *Atalanta*'s boats. And why would a ship's boat be covered with barnacles? Furthermore, deck beams in the water were not an uncommon sight in the North Atlantic following a stormy winter in the age of wooden ships.

Finally, in June 1880 two issues of *Vide Penny Illustrated Paper* carried "definite news" of the lost *Atalanta*. The paper reported that a fishing-vessel captain from Rockport, Massachusetts, had picked up a bottle that was floating about a mile offshore. A note in the bottle, "scrawled in apparent great haste," said that the training ship *Atalanta* was sinking on April 17 at longitude 270, latitude 32 degrees. That position is west of the Madeira Islands and south of the Azores—an unlikely place for the *Atalanta* to have been. The "scrawled" note was signed John L. Hutchings.

The second report in the illustrated paper was about a piece of barrel stave found by children on a beach near Halifax, Nova Scotia. A message was said to be scratched on the stave. It said: "*Atalanta* going down, April 15, 1880. No hope." The message was signed James White.

Neither report was taken very seriously at the time. And there was no record of either John Hutchings or James White on the *Atalanta*. In the 1920's, the renowned author and "ghost chaser" Elliot O'Donnell studied the disappearance of the *Atalanta*. And he concluded that both messages were fakes. Obviously these "messages" were based on the assumption that the *Atalanta* went down in the eastern Atlantic during the great mid-April storm. Mr. O'Donnell didn't think that the *Atalanta* ever reached the eastern part of the Atlantic. In his opinion, the ship was probably lost in a storm that swept through the mid-Atlantic in early February.

However, that storm would probably have been far north

of the *Atalanta*'s likely course by the time the ship reached that mid-Atlantic area. The ship left Hamilton on January 31, 1880. And since it was a broad-beamed frigate with shortened masts, it probably averaged no more than eight knots. So it seems unlikely that the training ship could have maneuvered around Bermuda and sailed a few hundred miles eastward into the path of the storm within a few days.

Many people who study mysteries of the sea are now inclined to think that the *Atalanta* was lost within the Bermuda Triangle. The ship was last seen leaving Hamilton Harbor on January 31, 1880. Following a common practice of the day, the training ship may have swung southward around the eastern tip of the main island of Bermuda to pick up the prevailing winds. That would have put the ship well into the Triangle.

Several ships were sailing westward to Bermuda in early February. None of them reported seeing the *Atalanta* or any trace of wreckage. When the *Atalanta* left Hamilton Harbor, it vanished from the face of the earth. And no trace of the training ship has ever been found.

11. Did the SS *Marine Sulphur Queen* Explode?

by Kent Jordan

The disappearance of the SS Marine Sulphur Queen, *a huge tanker filled with liquid sulphur, would seem, at first glance, a near-impossibility. Even if it blew up, because of its inflammable content, would not the cargo and remnants of the vessel create large wreckage and widespread noxious pollution of the sea? Mr. Jordan's summary of the views and events concerning the ship's disappearance is based on a report of the U.S. Coast Guard's Marine Board of Investigation and its subsequent review by Admiral E. J. Roland, then commandant, U.S. Coast Guard Headquarters, Washington, D.C. Supplementing this report is the full text of the investigating board's findings, which appears as an Appendix at the end of this book.*

85

THE SS *Marine Sulphur Queen* left Sabine Sea Buoy at Beaumont, Texas, at 6:30 P.M. on February 2, 1963. The vessel was expected to arrive in Norfolk, Virginia, five days later. It was last heard from on February 4 at 1:25 A.M.

No one knows precisely what happened to the ship, its crew of thirty-nine men, its cargo of 15,260 tons of molten sulphur, or most of its hulk, equipment and miscellaneous content.

When it became clear, on February 7, that the ship was overdue, the commander of the U.S. Coast Guard's Fifth District notified the Rescue Coordination Center in New York via a "hot line." That same day, an "All Ships Urgent Broadcast" was made for the location and rescue, if possible, of the missing ship. This broadcast was repeated until February 16. All efforts to contact the vessel by radio were fruitless.

On February 8, at 8:00 A.M., a surface and air search was begun, which followed this pattern:

February 8: A day search was undertaken, following a trackline from Beaumont through the Straits of Florida, a distance of 1,630 miles. Seven planes were used for this search, which covered about 58,000 miles. The search extended thirty miles on either side of the ship's assumed route.

February 8 and 9: Three planes undertook a night search during this period, making twenty-three flights in all and covering 22,000 square miles.

February 9: As the *Marine Sulphur Queen* had not been located on the route, or track, it was supposed to have taken, a much wider search was undertaken. In all, 95,000 miles were covered by nineteen planes, which flew a total number of 114 flight hours.

February 9 and 10: Another night search was undertaken after sunset, with two planes covering 8,300 square miles for a total of twelve flight hours.

February 10: Yet another day search took place. This time, nineteen planes flew 136 hours and searched an area of 76,700 square miles.

February 11: Fourteen planes undertook searches during daylight hours, covering 55,000 square miles in eighty-six flight hours.

February 12: Ten planes flew forty-two hours and searched 22,000 square miles.

February 13: In a final daylight search, two aircraft flew

sixteen flight hours and covered an area of 11,000 square miles.

Following this preliminary search in which Coast Guard, Marine Corps, and Air Force planes participated, it was concluded that the "negative results" indicated further, intensive searches by sea. In all, the planes had flown eighty-three sorties, flying nearly five hundred hours, and covered the vast area of close to 350,000 square miles. Meanwhile, the Coast Guard's Atlantic Merchant Vessel Reporting system got in touch with forty-two ships that could possibly have seen the *Marine Sulphur Queen* during the first days of its voyage. Nothing, however, emerged from these queries that threw any light on the vessel's course or fate.

The Marine Board of Investigation added:

"On 20 February, a U.S. Navy torpedo retriever boat operating about 12 miles southwest of Key West, Florida, sighted and picked up a fog horn and life jacket stencilled with the vessel's name. The second phase of the search for the MARINE SULPHUR QUEEN was then instituted, confined primarily to the area just west of Dry Tortugas Island, thence through the Straits of Florida, along the axis of the Gulf Stream, including the Bahamas Islands, and the east coast of Florida to Cape Canaveral. This search with seven ships and 48 aircraft sorties flying 271.4 hours covered an additional 59,868 square miles. The probability of sighting during both search phases was computed to be 95% for a vessel, 70% for a metal lifeboat and 65% for a liferaft.

"The U. S. Navy conducted an underwater search for the vessel's hulk during the period of 20 February through 13 March in an area from the shoals to the 100 fathom curve between Key West and 24°35′N, 83°30′W, using six Navy vessels for 523 hours on the scene and 17 aircraft sorties flying 57 hours with possibility of detection of 80% for the hulk. During this period, additional debris was recovered and identified as coming from the MARINE SULPHUR QUEEN. At 1740 [5:40 P.M.] EST, 14 March 1963, having received negative reports from all participating units, the search for the vessel was discontinued.

"The material recovered and identified as from the MARINE SULPHUR QUEEN consisted of 8 life jackets, 5 life rings, 2 name boards, 1 shirt, 1 piece of an oar, 1 storm oil can, 1 gasoline can, 1 cone buoy, and 1 fog horn. This material was deposited with the Coast Guard at Miami, Florida and later shipped to Washington, D.C. where it was examined by experts from the Bureau of Standards, the Coast Guard, and the Bureau of Fisheries. The consensus of opinion was that possibly two life jackets had been worn by persons and that the shirt tied to a life jacket had also been worn by a person. Numerous tears on the life jackets indicated attack by predatory fish. Further examination was made of certain of the debris by the Federal Bureau of Investigation who determined that the shirt bore no laundry marks, visible or invisible, and that no trace of sulphur particles was evident on any of the material. Visual examination of the material disclosed no trace of either explosion or fire.

"On 29 April 1963, the Coast Guard Air Detachment, Corpus Christi was given a note that was reported to have been in a whiskey bottle found on or before that date by a Spanish-speaking man in Laguna Madre, near Corpus Christi at approximate position 27°39.5′N, 97°15.4′W. The bottle was broken to get the note out. A search for pieces of the bottle at that time were negative. However, the Board received the bottom of the purported bottle with no sealife attached thereto on 13 June 1963. This note written with ball point pen on a piece of manila paper, similar to a paper bag, was unsigned and referred to an explosion and two men hurt. The piece of paper also had a crude map of the Gulf of Mexico, Florida Straits and Cuba with a circle surrounding an 'X', and the word 'SHIP.' This 'X' was near the western approach to the Florida Straits. The note was turned over to a Federal examiner of questioned documents who stated in his opinion, based upon crew signatures and a letter from one crew member to his sister, that it was written by a particular crew member."

The bottle, identified with one of the missing crew members, became an elusive element of evidence in locating the vessel and determining the sea and air conditions under which it had operated. The director of the Coast and Geodetic Survey concluded that it could not possibly have reached the Corpus Christi area, assuming it was dropped at any place east of 85 degrees west, "unless a strong southeasterly wind had been blowing for several days before and after the dropping." But winds, at that time, had been northerly.

The Coast Guard investigation concluded that the *Marine Sulphur Queen* had encountered "high and rough seas" on February 3 while in the Gulf of Mexico, and on February 4, while approaching the Straits of Florida. At 1:25 A.M.—in other words, in the early-morning hours—of February 4, the ship transmitted a personal message from a crew member to a shore point; however, near noon the same day, at 11:23

A.M., the ship could no longer be reached by radio, and all later efforts to do so failed. The investigative board concluded that "the vessel foundered sometime on 4 February 1963 on the approach to or in the vicinity of the Straits of Florida." It added, however, that "In view of the absence of any survivors and the physical remains of the vessel, the exact cause for the disappearance of the *Marine Sulphur Queen* could not be ascertained."

Chances are that the vessel exploded in the stormy seas, probably because of structural failures. There wasn't enough time to save the crew, because the few life jackets that were picked up were, the board assumed, probably worn by crew members who were on watch duty and thus "had them readily available." Whatever debris of the vessel was found had been drifting in the waters off the southern tip of Florida. The geodetic report on the message in the bottle made it doubtful that it was dropped into the sea before the vessel foundered—how could anyone have had the time to write the note, put it in the bottle, and tape the bottle shut, when there hadn't even been enough time to send out a radio distress signal?

While the Marine Board of Investigation refers to the assumption that an explosion tore the *Marine Sulphur Queen* apart as "conjecture," it nevertheless indicated such a disaster as a distinct possibility. Its report (*see* Appendix) goes into great detail concerning the construction of the vessel, which had been converted from an oil tanker to a sulphur-carrying vessel in such a way as to weaken it seriously. Divisions between the various sections of the ship had been removed, so that an explosion or other damage occurring in one section of the ship could immediately spread to the rest of the vessel.

Consequently, when Admiral Roland evaluated the board's findings, he noted that, in addition to the explosion hypothesis, it had also been considered that there had been "a complete failure of the vessel's hull girder," which "may have caused it to break in two." Further, the vessel may have "capsized in synchronous rolling" in high seas, or "a steam explosion may have occurred as the result of a rapid filling of the void space with water." The admiral agreed that future oil tankers should not be converted into sulphur tankers in the manner of the *Marine Sulphur Queen*, unless individual cases showed a particularly strong ship's body. After discussing the merits of other recommendations, the admiral stated: "Concurring in another of the board's recommendations, regulations are being developed for submission to the

89

Merchant Marine Council which would require operators of molten sulphur carriers to provide appropriate instructions and indoctrination for vessel personnel concerning hazards of molten sulphur cargoes." The inspection of such ships was to be stepped up, although, since then, few vessels carry molten sulphur.

The case of the SS *Marine Sulphur Queen* is in the category of the "Bermuda Triangle" mysteries only because the Marine Board of Investigation could not decide on the specific cause of the disaster, and because relatively few bits of debris could be found. It is cited by Charles Berlitz in his book *The Bermuda Triangle* in a chapter entitled "The Sea of Lost Ships." Berlitz identifies the last radio message from the vessel as that of a sailor who "had been speculating on the stock market, specifically in wheat futures, a pastime that normally requires rather close contact with one's broker." When the sailor's "buy" order, made before he left Beaumont, could not be confirmed by the brokerage firm—because radio contact could not be established—"the brokerage house informed the ship's owners that they could not reach the vessel." John Wallace Spencer, in *Limbo of the Lost,* summarized the *Marine Sulphur Queen* case factually, but asked: "Why are no lifeboats, oil slick, or floating sulphur found? Why was no distress signal sent?" He added that the boat "was written off" by the Coast Guard inquiry "as just one more unsolved mystery in the 'Limbo of the Lost.'" Richard Winer, in *The Devil's Triangle,* said that as the ship rounded the Florida Keys, "a crew member sent a radiogram to his wife, telling her of the expected arrival time in Norfolk," while another sailor "sent a radio message to his stockbroker in Tampa." This last reference is presumably another version of the speculation-in-wheat element in the wireless communications to and from the *Marine Sulphur Queen,* although it differs somewhat from Mr. Berlitz' account. Winer noted that almost every article and story on the Bermuda Triangle "includes the loss of the *Marine Sulphur Queen* as a strange mystery," and added that it appeared to be "nothing mysterious or supernatural—simply an industrial explosion at sea." Lawrence D. Kusche, in *The Bermuda Triangle Mystery—Solved,* devotes a chapter to the fate of the vessel. After quoting from Coast Guard reports, he wrote that "the legend of the Bermuda Triangle has it that the Coast Guard failed to find an explanation for the loss" of the ship, but points out that it listed four possible causes, and the commandant a fifth. Kusche also said:

"Widows and relatives of the men filed suit soon after the incident, asking damages from the owner of the ship. The legal battle has continued for more than ten years. On the tenth anniversary of the *Marine Sulphur Queen*'s disappearance it was announced that one of the first of the wrongful death claims had been settled, with court approval of an award of $115,000 to the widow of an ordinary seaman. In 1972 the Supreme Court let stand a lower court ruling that the ship was unseaworthy. Claims reported to total over $7 million may now be pressed. The rapid sinking of the ship prompted an investigation into the use of automatic emergency warning systems and position-indicating radio beacons."

One reason for paying special attention to the case of the SS *Marine Sulphur Queen*, within the context of the Bermuda Triangle mysteries, is the nature of its disappearance, together with the detailed information available concerning the vessel. The farther back an incident, the less reliable information we have; consequently, the more mysterious becomes the disappearance itself. In the case of this sulphur carrier, the data on the condition of the vessel itself are very detailed, and the extensive searches did result in locating such items as life jackets, no matter how few in number. In a sense, then, the *Marine Sulphur Queen* is a "classic" case of what might have been a highly mysterious disappearance—made a good deal less mysterious, although not totally conclusive, by the factual information available.

12. Did an Earthquake Wreck the *Freya*?

from Nature *magazine*

The German bark Freya *left the Cuban port city of Manzanillo on October 3, 1902, bound for Panta Arenas, Chile. Nothing was heard from the vessel until, twenty days later, the ship was found tilted to one side, with its masts partly destroyed, and abandoned by its crew. Charles Berlitz, writing in* The Bermuda Triangle *(1974), puts the* Freya *into the category of deserted ships that have, on numerous occasions, "inexplicably" appeared inside the Triangle area. He noted that "at this point in time a violent earthquake had taken place in Mexico" and that it "has been predicted" that a seismic shock caused "formation of a huge tidal wave which swept away the crew of the Freya or perhaps partially capsized it, and that it subsequently partially righted itself again when the sea was calm." The British scientific periodical Nature printed the following acccount of these events on April 25, 1907, placing them within the wider perspective of interrelated land and sea disasters.*

ANOTHER great earthquake has been added to the series which has marked the recent increase in seismic and volcanic activity along the Pacific coast of America. At 11:30 P.M. on Sunday, April 14, or about 6 A.M. of April 15 by Greenwich time, the greater part of Mexico was visited by a destructive earthquake. As usual, the first accounts were not only exaggerated, but gave an erroneous impression of the distribution of damage; Mexico City, which was represented as almost destroyed, proved by later accounts to have been comparatively little damaged; while the towns of Chilpancingo and Chilapu, as well as some others not to be found in ordinary atlases, suffered great destruction. The sea-coast towns from Salina Cruz to Acapulco suffered severely, and a portion of the latter is said to have been submerged. The shock is reported as severe at San Luis Potori and Juan Batista, though no damage was done at either place; these two cities are about 530 miles apart and about 350 miles from the region of greatest damage, so we may estimate the area over which the shock was sensible as extending to somewhere about 500 miles from the center of the disturbance.

The earliest reports stated that railway communication between Mexico city and Vera Cruz was suspended owing to the sinking of the permanent way, but this news, which has not been corrroborated in later telegrams, is the only suggestion that the focus of the earthquake may have extended to any distance from the west coast. Everything else points to the conclusion that it originated close to the shore-line of the Pacific, and was partly, if not wholly, submarine.

Sea-quakes are common in this region; sometimes they are felt by ships at sea though unnoticed on shore, and in at least one instance seem to have caused the loss of a ship. The story is a remarkable one. On October 3, 1902, the German barque *Freya* cleared from Manzanillo for Panta Arenas; nothing more has been heard of the captain or crew, but the ship was found, twenty days later, partially dismasted and lying on its side. There was nothing to explain the condition of the ship, but a wall calendar in the captain's cabin showed that the catastrophe must have overtaken it on October 4, not long after leaving port, as was also indicated by the anchor being found still hanging free at the bow.

Weather reports show that only light winds were experienced to this region from October 3 to October 5, but, on the other hand, severe earthquakes were felt at Acapulco and Chilpancingo on October 4 and 5, one of which probably caused the damage to the *Freya* which led to its abandonment.

Prominence has been given in the daily papers to earthquakes in Spain and Italy, which occurred shortly after the Mexican one; but they were of an order the occurrence of which is too frequent to justify any direct connection between them and the greater one. It may be different as regards the other two large earthquakes, which were registered at 9:10 P.M. on April 18, and at 12:11 A.M. on April 19; no news of these shocks has yet reached us; they must have been earthquakes of the first order of importance but are only known from distant records, which are interpreted as showing that they originated at about 90 degrees from western Europe. This is about the distance of Mexico, but it is rare for aftershocks to be of as great magnitude as these; on the other hand, it is not uncommon for earthquakes to take place in groups, usually originating at nearly opposite points in the globe. We may consequently, in the absence of news of a great earthquake in America or Japan, look for the origin of these two earthquakes in the North Pacific Ocean on the eastern part of the Malay Peninsula.

13. Cruise to Oblivion

by Allen Roberts

A fifty-four-foot trawler-yacht disappeared during its shakedown cruise in the Caribbean early in 1974. This is a recent, well-documented case, narrated here by a close observer of the preparations and background to the Saba Bank's mysteri-

ous disappearance. Here is a case that is concrete and dramatic in its contemporary, everyday detail.

"THEY did have some understanding of the sea. They didn't spend all their money on iceboxes and fancy appointments inside.

"They spent a good bit of money on the safety gear too. I don't think that they spared a dime on safety gear. If it was available and useful, they bought it.

"That's the part that makes it so incredible. . . ."

Captain Larry Menkes's voice trailed off as he expressed again his bafflement at what happened to the *Saba Bank*, the fifty-four-foot trawler-yacht that disappeared on a shakedown cruise of the Caribbean in March 1974.

The yacht left Nassau March 10. It was scheduled to arrive at Dinner Key marina in Coconut Grove just south of Miami about April 8. Then it was to be charted out by its owner, the Vaco Corporation of Wilmington, Delaware. But the *Saba Bank* sailed into oblivion. Nothing was heard from it from the time it left Nasssau Yacht Haven.

Aboard the *Saba Bank* were the skipper, thirty-two-year-old Cy Zenter of Philadelphia, and his cousins Elliott Cohen, thirty, also of Philadelphia, and Raphael Kaplan, twenty-six, of Sicklerville, New Jersey. They were accompanied by a friend, John Tarquinio, forty-two, of Vineland, New Jersey.

The $300,000 yacht had a complete array of navigation and communication gear—VHF and FM radios, radar, and emergency beacons. But the powerful radios remained silent. April 8 came and went, but there was no word from the *Saba Bank*.

The Coast Guard station in Miami was alerted, and on April 10 the Coast Guard began a radio search throughout the Caribbean. Urgent messages were sent out daily in hopes of raising the yacht or learning of its whereabouts.

There was still no answer.

The Vaco Corporation hired Menkes, a Miami charter-yacht captain who knew and had sailed with Zenter and had gone to school with the older brother of Elliott Cohen, to coordinate the search and rescue efforts. Menkes and representatives of Vaco hired a plane and made an extensive aerial search, concentrating on areas that wouldn't normally be covered by the Coast Guard and checking the fringes of the areas in which the *Saba Bank* was expected to be.

The Coast Guard did not make an active search itself, but its ships and planes were alerted to be on the lookout for the

Saba Bank while on routine patrol and while searching for other lost vessels.

Menkes remained confident for some time.

"It's probably adrift without power somewhere far out of the shippping lanes," he said in late April. "Sooner or later it will turn up. But it's a big ocean, and it could be weeks and weeks yet."

Weeks and weeks passed, and then months and months, but there was still no word on the missing yacht. Rumors, yes. Scores of them.

"They called me search coordinator, but I was really 'rumor central,' " Menkes says wryly now.

A fifty-four-foot yacht—described by Captain Menkes as strong and seaworthy and "incredibly well equipped: long-distance radio capability, rescue locator beacons, radar, the works"—and the four men aboard her had vanished. What happened to her?

"I wish I had a theory," Menkes says ruefully. "We worked long and hard on this and came up with precious little."

There have been numerous explanations offered for the all-too-frequent disappearances of ships and planes within the Devil's Triangle, that area bounded roughly by Miami, Puerto Rico, and Bermuda that carries such a freight of myth and legend.

The Coast Guard, officially at least, believes that there is nothing mysterious about the frequent disappearances. All, or nearly all, can be explained by the turbulent waters and violent weather encountered in the Triangle. And, indeed, the weather in the semitropical region that includes Florida and its surrounding waters can be vicious.

The region is the victim of more thunderstorms than almost anywhere else in the world. Parts of Florida average more than one hundred a year. One pilot counted thirteen thunderstorms during an hour-and-a-half flight between Lakeland in central Florida and Fort Lauderdale on the east coast.

The area's warm, moist, and unstable air is a perfect breeder of the violent storms that can measure ten miles across at the base and tower to a height of forty thousand feet. Several storms can develop together in clusters known as squall lines, which can extend hundreds of miles.

They build with deceptive speed. A calendar-beautiful sky can turn black within minutes as a thunderstorm builds to gigantic size and lashes the land and oceans with torrents of rain and near-hurricane-force winds.

Did the *Saba Bank* founder in a thunderstorm or squall line?

Even though he has noted that the yacht's crew wasn't very experienced at all, Captain Menkes doesn't believe that the boat was sunk by a storm. The weather was generally good, he noted. "There was some squally weather during the period, but not anything that would disturb that kind of yacht.

"She was really well built; probably more seaworthy than most of the boats that go out.

"She was strong enough to survive almost anything."

Moreover, it's hard to imagine a storm striking so fast that the crew never got off a distress call. There is a feature of thunderstorms that could possibly destroy a boat without warning under some circumstances. Lightning has been known to destroy boats and planes by exploding gas fumes from leaky fittings or gas tanks. The region's thunderstorms are such a fruitful source of lightning that investigators frequently conduct their research there.

In the early 1960's Dr. Bernard Vonnegut of the State University of New York and Charles Moore of the New Mexico Institute of Mining and Technology rigged up a sophisticated array of instruments on Grand Bahama Island to test and ultimately help prove a theory that it is the lightning in a thunderstorm that triggers the rain. And in 1966 Dr. M. M. Newman and co-workers of the Lightning and Transients Research Institute took a research vessel named the *Thunderbolt* into Florida waters in a lightning experiment involving firing of wire-carrying rockets into thunderheads.

The awesome power of lightning displays in the Devil's Triangle was vividly attested to by a Fort Lauderdale sailor named Bill Verity. Verity made two one-man voyages across the Atlantic to test a theory that Saint Brendan and his Irish monks could have sailed the Atlantic in the sixth century. On his second trip, in 1969—from Ireland to Fort Lauderdale—Verity sailed his twenty-foot wooden sloop through an electrical storm that transfixed him.

"I was so scared that I didn't know what to do. Lightning was hitting all around—so close that I could smell it. . . ."

Lightning is believed to have been a factor in several plane and boat disasters in the past. More than seventy witnesses reported seeing lightning strike a Pan American Airways Boeing 707 near Elkton, Maryland, in 1963 just before it plunged like a fiery comet into an open field, killing more than eighty people.

Lightning was also responsibile for a near-disaster in the space program when a bolt struck a manned Apollo spaceship seconds after liftoff, momentarily disrupting most of the vital electronic gear on board.

Tornadoes and waterspouts are another troublesome off-spring of thunderstorms, capable of inflicting severe damage on boats and planes or even destroying them. Waterspouts are so common in the area that people on shore can sometimes see two or more at a time twisting their way across the water.

While waterspouts are usually visible for miles and easily avoidable, a ship could blunder into one at night or in poor visibility.

But if the *Saba Bank* had died in an explosion, lightning-induced or not, or had been ripped apart by a waterspout, there would have been considerable wreckage. The yacht had two life rafts, each of which was attached with hydrostatic releases that would automatically free them if the yacht sank. Each life raft was equipped with an emergency locator beacon that would produce a signal that a rescue vessel or plane could home in on.

It's a big ocean but a busy one, crisscrossed by hundreds of boats and planes each week. But no wreckage of the *Saba Bank* was ever reported. Nevertheless, the size of the ocean can awe even a veteran sailor like Captain Menkes: "I spent enough time flying over the ocean out there to realize how hard it is to find even a big ship. So a small life raft could be drifting out there right now.

"They say some debris from wreckage that occurred right here in the Gulf Stream has washed ashore on the north coast of Ireland and the North Sea countries three years later," Menkes adds.

The Gulf Stream itself can be an instrument of destruction.

"I have seen the Gulf Stream when it's riled up, an incredible body of water," Menkes says. "It's hard to believe how nasty it can get out in the Gulf Stream, almost unbelievably nasty. It's enough to give you a nightmare, and I'm sure it's been responsible for a number of missing boats.

"But," he goes on, "I should think that that particular boat would have survived pretty much anything that the Gulf Stream could have dished out."

One theory that got considerable attention was that the *Saba Bank* might have been a victim of hijackers seeking boats with the speed and size to be used for smuggling narcotics. Prior to the opening of hearings by the House Merchant Marine and Fisheries Committee in August 1974, Congressman John Murphy claimed that hundreds of boat owners and crews have disappeared and are believed victims of drug runners.

Murphy said that heroin and marihuana smugglers commandeer yachts on the high seas, kill the occupants, and then use the yacht as contraband cutters. After a few fast runs, the boats are frequently scuttled, according to a report Murphy prepared for the committee hearings.

"Literally hundreds of boats and hundreds of owners and crews have disappeared in the southeastern Atlantic, the Gulf of Mexico, along the Pacific Coast, and in Hawaii. The great bulk of the victims were actual or suspected targets of drug smugglers," the report said.

Murphy's report was criticized by some Coast Guard officials as an overstatement. And Bill Stevens, involved for nearly twenty-five years in Caribbean yachting, called the report grossly exaggerated. "To our knowledge, there have been maybe two or three such cases."

But one Coast Guard official testified at the House hearings that as many as thirty yachts may have been hijacked. Coast Guard Commander M. K. Phillips, senior duty officer at the Coast Guard Operations Center in Washington, testified that only four cases of piracy by drug runners have been documented in the past three years, but added: "The possibility that as many as thirty more vessels may have fallen victim to hijackers or pirates cannot be discounted despite the lack of hard evidence."

The *Saba Bank* was specifically mentioned as a possible hijack victim in Murphy's report to the committee. At the time of the hearings, the Miami Coast Guard office had a list of twenty-two documented cases of missing boats or crews.

"We don't know what happened to them," said Commander James Webb, public-affairs assistant chief for Coast Guard headquarters in Washington.

"They all had one or more elements, however, conducive to hijacking," he said. Those factors are, he noted, that: the boat was very seaworthy; it was outfitted for a long trip; the operators had taken along unfamiliar crewmen.

While the last factor wasn't present in the case of the *Saba Bank*, the other two definitely were, and Ned Rogovoy, an attorney for Vaco Corporation, indicated that he hoped the yacht had been hijacked. "I know everybody around here is hoping it was—that way there's a chance those aboard are still alive."

If the *Saba Bank* was indeed hijacked, that hope would appear to be slim. At any rate, Menkes doesn't think it likely. While conceding that "the boat would have been a prize for anybody," Menkes notes that the Vaco Corporation had offered a substantial reward for information about the *Saba Bank*, starting at $2,500 and eventually raised to $20,000.

"I think that if it was a case of dirty doings, someone would have come up with some information on it," he said.

There have, of course, been other theories advanced to explain mysterious disappearances in the Devil's Triangle—UFO's, time and space warps, and such. And reports of strange events still surface on occasion. A Palm Beach pilot told a reporter about a flight from Freeport in the Bahamas to Palm Beach during which he appeared to enter a black tunnel that extended as far as he could see backward and forward.

The pilot, a veteran of hundreds of flights over the area, said that his watch apparently stopped and his instruments went crazy. He doesn't know how long he was in the tunnel, and he was baffled by the phenomena. Baffled and a bit scared, and maybe a little embarrassed. At any rate, until he talked to the reporter about two years after the incident, he had never told anyone about it. Fatigue? A form of self-hypnosis?

Perhaps, but the pilot's report is only one of dozens and perhaps even hundreds of strange incidents recorded in the twilight zone known as the Devil's Triangle. And as long as boats like the *Saba Bank* keep disappearing without a trace, no theory can be completely ruled out.

Menkes admits he's baffled. "I don't know. I just don't have a theory that explains it."

14. "I Don't Want to be Another Statistic!"

The Adventure of Captain Don Henry

What, exactly, happened to Captain Henry's 160-foot tug, the Good News, *when it was traveling through the Bermuda Triangle area on a perfectly calm, clear day in 1966? The electric energy was drained out of his equipment, the sea around the tug was a milky foam, there seemed no horizon to separate it from the sky, and the huge barge the tug was pulling had completely disappeared. Some marine specialists suggest that a waterspout may have turned the sea into a white caldron, while temporarily separating tug and barge. But the captain rejects such explanations. The twelve minutes, one afternoon, in the center of a Caribbean mystery have, as he puts it, "made a believer" out of him.*

ONE of the most knowledgeable contemporary witnesses of a mystery event in the so-called Bermuda Triangle area has been Captain Don Henry, who owns a salvage company in Miami, the Sea Phantom Exploration Company. But since a mysterious force manipulated his tug, the *Good News*, back in 1966, he has had the ambition of exploring the Triangle area thoroughly by electronic means, although he has calculated that such an expedition "might well take about eighteen months" to cover the necessary territory and will require special equipment.

Captain Don Henry told his unnerving adventure story to a nationwide television audience early in 1975, when he and a group of other advocates and adversaries appeared on the David Susskind panel show. Also on the program was author Charles Berlitz, who had quoted Henry's account in his book *The Bermuda Triangle*, where he identifies the captain as having had "many years' experience as a sea captain, navigator, and both a hard hat and free diver." He described him as in his mid-fifties, with "a powerful chest and arms befitting a long-time diver," who is "extremely solid and muscular and, for a heavy man, moves with surprising lightness and speed."

Among the panel members, Don Henry stood out as the most plain-spoken and least theoretical, and appeared to be almost reflexively nautical in personality. He started speaking of his adventure by saying that the *Good News* was on its way from Puerto Rico to the Miami–Fort Lauderdale area, manned by a crew of twenty-three, plus the captain himself. The tug, towing a heavy barge, was three days out of Puerto Rico, when, in the Bermuda Triangle area, it had what Captain Henry called a "weird experience." He said: "I had gone to my cabin, which is just after the bridge. I had gone for a little rest; I had been on the bridge for some time. While I was in my cabin, there was a good deal of commotion on the bridge. People started hollering and screaming, and I went out to ask them what was going on.

"The chief officer was on the bridge, and he said, 'Take a look at the compass, Cap.' I walked over and looked. The gyro was spinning in a clockwise motion, and the magnetic compass had gone completely bananas. I had never seen anything like it before. I know a compass can tumble, but not on a boat, where it just doesn't get the acceleration for that much motion. The magnetic compass was just simply going around and around. A magnetic compass points toward true north, from the magnetic pole; a gyro compass sets up its own magnetic field and points north.

"We checked later for any power flux that might have influenced the compass, but there had been none. We keep a constant watch on our generator, to guard against that sort of thing. It was somewhat cloudy, but we did not have cumulus clouds. The clouds were high up. There was no storm. The weather was flat calm.

"I went out on the bridge, just to take a look around. There was no horizon; there was no sky. You couldn't see where the water ended and the sky began. It looked as if there was no ocean. It was all one. You looked down on the water, and what you saw was foam, you saw milk. The sky was the same color, and so there was no horizon, no definition between the two, as there otherwise always is. And when I looked back at the barge we were towing—there was no barge! We had felt no snap. The towline was there. It was still leading over the aft, the way it was supposed to be, but there was no barge. If a barge that size had been severed from a tug pulling with all its power, you'd take off like a scalded cat.

"I ran to the afterdeck of the tug, went on the ladder down under the towing deck, and started to pull the line. Not that I wanted to, or could have, pulled the barge; but I wanted to feel the barge on the line. There was weight there, all right.

"And a few minutes later—here comes the barge, right back into existence again. There was no fog around us, but there seemed to be fog around the barge. Still, the weather was clear. You could see a good eleven miles before this happened. The barge came back. I had kicked the throttles of the boat forward, because all I could think of at the time was, 'Let's get out of here, I don't want to be another statistic!' So we left, and kept plowing ahead.

"But it seemed that something was pulling us back while we were trying to go ahead. And I didn't know what it was, and I was hoping that the towline, which was three-and-a-half-inch, wouldn't part. If you've spent any time at sea, you can tell when your ship is moving and when it's restrained. There is a vibration in the ship that is there all the time, but you can feel what the ship is doing. The whole thing took about twelve minutes from the time I stepped onto the bridge and the time the barge came back into view.

"I wanted to find out what had happened. So I put a boat over the side immediately, as soon as we got out of that spot, and went back to the barge. The barge was warm, much warmer than it should have been. It wasn't hot; you could touch it. But much warmer than would have been normal.

"There also was an electric drain during this period. We had no communication of any kind on the radios. There were no lights. The generators were running, but produced no energy. There was nothing. I had fifty flashlight batteries that were completely drained. We had to throw them away. It was a case of batteries that I had bought in Puerto Rico."

Mr. Susskind, referring to Captain Henry as "the quintessential sea dog, tough and knowing and expert," asked him, "Do you believe something extraordinary happened?"

The captain answered: "It scared the hell out of me, but it didn't make me leery about going back down in that Bermuda Triangle again. If it did, I wouldn't sail anymore. Really! I mean, it's the thing that happened, and it made a 'believer' out of me. I do want to investigate it with my own company, making a full electronic search.

"Of my twenty-three men on the crew, all attest to what I saw, except the six that were sleeping. Seventeen men were on duty, and they all agree with what I saw."

Mr. Berlitz, quoting Captain Henry in his book, noted that the incident occurred in a spot known as "the Tongue of the

Ocean," a submarine canyon within the Bahama group of islands, where the sea is about six hundred fathoms deep. The barge being towed weighed twenty-five hundred tons. The towline was some thousand feet long. Henry told Berlitz he knew of only one area where similar phenomena are recorded, in the Saint Lawrence River at Kingston, Canada, "where a big deposit of iron or maybe a meteorite on the bottom makes the compass go crazy." Also, while the energy drain was taking place on the *Good News* and the tug was unable to receive power from its generator, the engineer unsuccessfully tried to start an auxiliary generator, "but couldn't get a spark."

A reverse situation was encountered in the Tongue of the Ocean area by Joe Talley, captain of the shark-fishing boat the *Wild Goose*. His boat was being towed by another vessel, the *Caicos Trader*. Berlitz gives this account of what followed: "It was nighttime and Captain Talley was asleep in his bunk below decks. Suddenly he was awakened by a flood of water pouring over him. He automatically grabbed a life jacket and fought his way to an open porthole. As he forced his way out, he found he was under water but he encountered a line and followed it to the surface, a distance calculated as being from fifty to eighty feet."

Apparently, an unexplained force had pulled the *Wild Goose* under water. This pull threatened the towing ship, so the crew of the *Caicos Trader* cut the towline linking the two vessels. The towing vessel then circled back and was able to rescue Talley. The crew said they had seen the fishing boat go down, "as if in a whirlpool."

Except for the coincidences that both events took place in the Tongue of the Ocean, and that in each case the towing of one ship by another was involved, the two mysterious incidents have little in common. The various elements described by Captain Henry all point to a unique combination of forces acting in concert during a relatively short period of time. The draining of energy, the disturbance of the sea, and the malfunctioning of the compasses all point to an extremely odd constellation.

The spontaneity of such mixed phenomena makes them difficult to examine, as Captain Henry intended, by scientifically acceptable means. To begin with, even in the case of the *Good News,* independent depositions by crew members should be on record, together with logs and other documentation concerning the nature and condition of the two vessels, so as to establish a framework within which further investigation could proceed.

As for the actual examination of an area, such as the Tongue of the Ocean, a measuring of magnetic and other forces would seem to be the first requirement. The basic geological construction of the seabed and the nature of currents peculiar to the area, as well as related elements, would have to be fully studied to provide a foundation for further inquiry. No doubt, dealing with a more restricted area within the Bermuda Triangle, such as this particular submarine canyon, might be more feasible than research taking in a wider geographic area.

III

FANTASIES,
GUESSES, AND
CERTAINTIES

15. Of Time and the Triangle

by James Raymond Wolfe

Many of the Bermuda Triangle mysteries raise questions on points that seem to do violence to our ideas of what can and cannot happen in our physical universe. Yet ... is this really so?

Man has made great strides toward understanding the nature of the cosmos of which he is a part. But many of his discoveries are so far removed from commonplace experience that they remain almost exclusively the property of the relativistic philosopher and the quantum physicist. They are practically unknown to the man in the street.

For instance: like most informed adults, you probably understand that there are two kinds of electricity—positive and negative. However, in the world of the semiconductor physicist, this is not so. To him negative electricity is the only kind there is. What you know of as positive electricity is no more than a flow of holes in space-time where negative electricity ought to be but isn't!

Furthermore, such a physicist will tell you that if such is not the true nature of electricity, then the transistors in your stereo equipment simply do not work.

In the far-out world of contemporaneous physics, matter is more of an experience than a substance, things can exist in two or more places at the same time, or they can go from hither to yon without crossing the space in between, and time itself can run backward.

Such phenomena are the particular field of study of our next author, James Raymond Wolfe. Educated at Loyola College and Johns Hopkins University, Mr. Wolfe is an erstwhile lecturer in paranormal phenomena at Clark University. In the following article, edited from a segment of one of his course lectures, he explores the possibility that some of the lesser-known principles of physics may underlie certain Bermuda Triangle mysteries.

. . . Now, so far we've looked at a few of the paradoxes that suggest time is not quite the stable, inexorably flowing stream that tradition considers it to be. Let's see if literature offers us any instances that might tend to demonstrate that.

Right now I'm going to talk about something that is a source of distress to travel agents, a certain fabulous vacation area that suffers from a peculiar affliction. With an eerie frequency, ships and planes and people disappear within its precincts, and no trace of them is ever seen again.

I refer to an area of sea off our southeastern coast known as the Bermuda Triangle.

The Triangle is drawn differently by various authorities, but most agree that it contains the area that is outlined when a line is drawn from Florida to Bermuda, from thence south to Puerto Rico, and then back, by way of the Bahamas, to Florida again.

Mysterious events in that area date back to before this country was discovered—four hours before, as a matter of fact. For at 10:00 P.M. on the night of October 11, 1492, Christopher Columbus and some others, on the deck of the *Santa Maria,* looked out over the ocean sea and saw a light. It looked like the flame of a candle that was being raised and lowered.

The problem facing historians is that the light was in a place where no light could have been. The ocean at that point is two and a half miles deep. The nearest land is thirty-five miles away, far beyond the range of a native canoe. There were only two other ships in the Western Hemisphere at the time, and Columbus could account for them.

Then what was the light that he and his officers saw?

Let's defer that question for the time. We'll get back to it later. Right now I want to take up a more recent Triangle mystery.

The *Star Tiger* was a passenger plane belonging to British-South American Airways. It served a route extending from London to the Azores, then Bermuda, and finally Havana. On the night from January 29 to 30, 1948, it was on the Azores–Bermuda leg of its course.

At 10:30 P.M. its pilot, Captain David Colby, radioed the tower at Hamilton, Bermuda, that he was running an hour and a half late due to strong headwinds. He said he would reach Hamilton at 1:00 A.M. and gave his position as 440 miles northeast of Bermuda.

But 1:00 A.M. came and went. The Hamilton tower found it could not contact the *Star Tiger.* No immediate alarm was felt, since the plane had fuel enough to last until 3:15 A.M. Moreover, the plane was pressurized and, in effect, hermetically sealed. If it had to be ditched in the ocean, it could be expected to float until all on board were safe on life rafts. As the water temperature was 65 degrees, not even anyone who was unlucky enough to be immersed suffered from any threat of freezing.

The life rafts were equipped with all the standard distress signaling equipment: flares, dye markers, and portable hand-cranked radio transmitters that could be heard at the low end of the AM broadcast band.

Despite this, and despite the largest air-sea search in history—200,000 square miles—nothing of the *Star Tiger* or its thirty-two passengers was ever seen again. A subsequent court of inquiry appointed by Britain's minister of civil aviation concluded that it could do no more "than suggest possibilities, none of which reaches the level even of probability. What happened in this case will never be known."

Five nights later, though, something happened that ties in with other events that have been recorded in the field of paranormal phenomena. Dismissed as a hoax at the time, it holds internal evidence that suggests it was anything but.

All through the night of February 3, radio amateurs all the way from Florida to Nova Scotia picked up signals that spelled out *s-t-a-r* and *s-t-a-r—t-i-g-e-r*. The signals ceased before direction finders could be brought to bear on them.

There were certain oddities about the signals. First, they were not sent in the international Morse code, nor did they make use of any standard distress calls, such as SOS or Mayday. They were tapped out in a contrived code in which one dot stood for *a*, two dots for *b*, down to twenty dots for *t*.

Furthermore, though the signals were sent by telegraph key, they were transmitted on the band used for *voice* distress signals.

This fits the case of a distressed person, ignorant of the standard code alphabet and distress signals, knowing nothing of radio equipment, who picked up a telegraphy key and plugged it into the wrong one of two jacks on a radio transmitter, sending out the only kind of code message he could think of.

Was this a survivor on the *Star Tiger*?

First let's see what aviation authorities said. They all agreed that, even sealed as it was, it was impossible that the aircraft could float for five days. They were just as much in agreement on another point: the heavy transmitting equipment aboard the *Star Tiger* could not have been carried onto a life raft.

Thus the aircraft was not afloat and its radio gear was not aboard a life raft. Since the air-sea search had covered land areas as well, it is just as certain that it had not pancaked on a beach.

The evidence suggests, then, that the *Star Tiger,* though neither on land or sea nor in the air, was, as far as its radio equipment was concerned, *intact at some point in space and time.*

All right. Let's put that case on the shelf for a few minutes and take up an analogous one that happened in Gallatin, Tennessee, sixty-eight years before.

David Lang was a farmer with a wife and two children, a boy and girl. Late in the afternoon of September 23, 1880, he sat on his porch with his family. Down the road, in full sight of the family, rode two friends in a buggy. They, in turn, could see Lang and his family.

Lang got up to bring in the horses from a nearby close-cropped, treeless pasture.

As he walked across the pasture, in full view of five witnesses, he simply disappeared!

He was there one minute, and in an instant, he was suddenly not there. Simply gone.

A month-long investigation, which included sounding the field for hidden holes, proved fruitless. Lang was never seen again.

Then, in early August of the next year, Lang's boy and girl were walking in the pasture. As they passed near the spot where Lang had vanished, the girl called out, "Father, are you anywhere around?"

And Lang's voice was heard, as if calling from a great distance: "Help!"

The children called their mother, who also called out to her husband. Lang's voice was heard over and over for the next three days, continually calling for help.

No one could tell the direction the voice came from, but all agreed that it seemed to get farther and farther away. Finally, it was heard no more.

There have been several other such cases. I have read of one that occurred a few years after Lang's; just outside of London, Scotland Yard men heard the voice of a vanished girl weeping that she "couldn't find the hole."

And what of the case of the "Green Children" chronicled by Ralph of Coggeshall in the year 1207? According to Coggeshall's *Chronicon Anglicarum*, two children found in Norfolk, England, told of emerging into this world through a hole that they were unable to locate again. In their world, they said, there was perpetual twilight. This suggests that they came from a high latitude on a planet that was not tilted on its axis like those of our solar system.

But let's look at the analogies between Lang's case and that of the *Star Tiger*. In the first place, there is a disappearance. Then a signal or voice is heard long after it would be physically possible to generate such a signal or voice. That is, the *Star Tiger* could not have survived, and Lang would certainly have starved to death. But let's see how these cases can be viewed in terms of time.

We saw previously that there are a number of ways of considering time. But for our present purpose, let's be simplistic and restrict ourselves to a concept of time as a dimension of duration. Even more simplistically, call it the distance between two events.

Take the case of Lang. The normal duration distance between September 1880 and August 1881 is measured as eleven months. *Suppose, then, with Lang, that for only an instant, duration ceased and the distance between September and August was reduced to zero.*

In that event, his wife and children would have heard him calling for help in what was the moment of his peculiar plight, but in what for them was the end of a duration period of eleven months.

We can illustrate this by a figure from topology, the Moebius Band. We take a strip of paper, give it a half-twist, and glue its ends together. Now we mark an X to show the location of Lang and his family in September 1880.

Taking a pencil, we carefully draw a line parallel to both sides, going halfway around the strip until we come to the part of the paper directly under the X. We will call that pencil track eleven months. Now, with a pin, we will poke a hole in the paper just where the X is.

The penciled track represents the path of Lang's family through eleven months and brings them around to the same relative area of the part in space, though it represents a journey along a duration track. The pinhole represents Lang's track.

Our paper must have substance to be seen. But suppose it to be infinitely thin. Then Lang's track through time, but in the same space, is zero. But his family's track is eleven months. Their track, however, is at right angles to his. If he

111

is still moving, he is getting farther away from them in time, though he may still be at the same space.

It is quite impossible to visualize this, but I ask you to imagine the usual 3-D space given a half-turn, as was given to the paper strip. Lang merely fell through the narrow side of that space, its duration dimension. His family took the long way around.

Now, returning to the *Star Tiger*, we find that our analogy holds. We may assume that it crashed onto the sea, but also into a new direction of duration. It remained afloat long enough for a survivor to tap out his laborious message. But he did not know that he had arrived at February 3 in an instant, whereas it would take five days for everyone else.

The *Star Tiger* is not the only plane to have disappeared under such unusual circumstances. Eleven months later, on December 18, 1948, a chartered DC-3 vanished within sight of Miami Airport, having all but completed a flight from San Juan, Puerto Rico. Though it was over shallow waters, no trace of it was ever found. The *Star Dust*, sister ship of the *Star Tiger*, disappeared from the skies in the same way within visual sighting distance of the airport at Santiago, Chile. Its last signal was sent twelve minutes before scheduled landing time. The *Star Dust* disappeared a year after the *Star Tiger*.

Now, if we assume a time displacement in these cases, then what causes it?

Well, we know of time reversals that can occur. For instance, if the electrical charge on every subatomic particle of an object were reversed at once, the object would recede from us in time, according to Richard P. Feynman of Cal Tech. For his findings he earned the Einstein Medal in 1953 and the Nobel Prize in 1965.

Unfortunately for us, the conditions under which a Feynman reversal would occur would also convert an object into antimatter. On contact with ordinary matter, both would blow up in a mammoth scintillation of gamma rays.

But there is another possibility. An object of imaginary mass could travel at a speed faster than light. Such an imaginary mass is a commonplace concept in quantum physics. But how could an aircraft be converted to imaginary mass and at the same time be given an acceleration to greater than the speed of light? Obviously the very idea raises more questions than it solves.

What we need, if we are going to explain such events as the *Star Tiger* and David Lang, is something that can distort space-time in a limited area and for an extremely short, practically imaginary unit of time.

Now, I'll admit that what I am about to suggest is speculative. Yet it does not lie outside the probability limitations of quantum physics.

The earth is continually bombarded by particles from outer space. I do not know exactly how many different types have been identified, but some of them have very peculiar characteristics. Take the neutrino, for example, with its zero charge and zero rest mass and no reaction to gravity; it has virtually no physical properties at all. Yet it exists in vast numbers.

I would propose a particle or an aggregation of particles, traveling just a hair under the speed of light. Their mass would then approximate the infinite. An aggregation of such particles would be extremely small due to being shrunk by the massive gravitational fields of its components.

The transition of such a particle through space-time would produce the Moeblus twist that we need. This according to Einstein's gravitational theory, that the greater the mass, the more distortion in ambient space-time.

With a particle almost infinitely small, but having an almost infinite mass, the volume of space distorted would be small, and so would be the dimension of time. But we do not need a great time distortion, just enough to nudge the target hit a little further ahead of us on the time track. Or maybe a little behind us.

If such particles occasionally drill into us from outer space, probability tells us that one or some of them will inevitably hit a plane or a ship or a person, knocking it out of its time orbit.

It would not surprise me if something like that happens in the Bermuda Triangle. And in other places of the world as well.

But to swing full circle back to Columbus' light . . .

Can't you see some poor doomed plane-crash survivor, huddled in his life raft, raising and lowering his waterproof cigarette lighter to see if its feeble illumination will throw any light on the three strange vessels that look so much like history-book representations of the *Pinta,* the *Nina,* and the *Santa Maria*?

16. Is the Triangle the Road to a Black Hole?

by Joseph F. Goodavage

Are people who disappear inside the Bermuda Triangle like so many fish being scooped out of an aquarium? Are they being sucked into a "Black Hole," the latest and most awesome discovery of modern astronomy? Mr. Goodavage cites the inexplicable disappearances of individuals and fits their fate into a pattern that may govern the mystery of the Triangle itself. He speculates that "infinitesimally small gravitational anomalies" exist and that people may be pulled into such areas, sucked into "another part of the universe or another dimension." A former newspaperman, Joseph F. Goodavage is the author of many articles and books, among them Astrology: The Space-Age Science *and* Write Your Own Horoscope.

Is THE force behind the many disappearances in the Atlantic Ocean *selective*? If not, why don't *all* ships and aircraft that pass over or through the so-called Bermuda Triangle disappear? Is it possible that for these disappearances to occur there must be a congress of unknown forces or energies? It may be a new kind of gravitational anomaly triggered by a combination of extraterrestrial forces that affect physical objects and influence human psychic and mental energy.

And human bodies.

It's one thing when ships and aircraft disappear. When the vessels are found intact, however, with no trace of passengers or crew, that's a whole 'nother ball game. That this has happened so often (in various places around the world) is well-documented. We may be dealing with an absolutely mind-boggling law of nature—or something even more astonishing.

If it's an undiscovered natural law, it seems to be intimately connected with certain previously unsuspected laws of gravity combined with the force or energy that governs telepathic communications (*not necessarily of the human vari-*

114

ety). The two phenomena give every indication of being intimately related.

We'll concentrate here on *human* disappearances—either alone or when their abandoned vessels have been found—for which there is no rational explanation.

According to Albert Einstein's close collaborator, the Nobel-prize-winning physicist Pascal Jordan, "A strong relationship exists between gravity and the force or energy that transmits telepathy."

Is there a common "telepathetic attunement" among those who have disappeared—in or near some gravitational anomaly—in the Bermuda Triangle or in other areas? If so, it's possible that the equation is made even more complex by the existence of certain other "wild variables," such as the constantly shifting positions of the planets, which cause the ever-changing center of gravity of the solar system.

Normally, because of our local star's stupendous size and its gravitational influence over its retinue of planets, the reciprocal effect of the planets on the Sun would seem to be infinitesimal—almost insignificant. But when giants like Jupiter and Saturn align on one side of the Sun, for example (especially when other planets of large mass are in opposition), great magnetic vortices rip through the photosphere and are often visible as sunspots and solar flares.

Sometimes the center of gravity of the entire system lies at the very core of the Sun. The center of gravity can also cruise with fantastic velocity (at depths of 300,000 miles or more) through the star's inner mass, or tear up the photosphere and whip far out into space, often engulfing the inner planets. This is the *mechanistic* explanation of gravity and its solar-planetary interaction (which, incidentally, affects the Earth's weather, seismic and volcanic activity, *and* the way human beings think, feel, and behave). But there's another, more subtle relationship between gravity (or, as some scientists now believe, new kinds of energy particles called "gravitons"—*i.e.*, miniature black holes) and telepathy.

"Gravity and telepathy have this in common," said Pascal Jordan; "they operate at great distances and cannot be barred by obstacles." At present, we can only speculate about the emotional and psychic state of those who have vanished from this world.

In December 1920, a five-masted, 3,500-ton American schooner, the *Carroll A. Deering*, sailed out of Portland, Maine, headed for Rio de Janeiro. She usually plied the trade routes between Portland and Barbados, so it wasn't unusual for her to head that far south.

On the return trip with a new cargo, she was cleared for Norfolk, Virginia, and scheduled to stop over at Barbados, where no change in her orders was forthcoming, so she sailed for Norfolk. By January 29 the *Deering*'s skipper, Captain Willis B. Wormwell, contacted the Cape Lookout lightship off North Carolina, and asked that the G. G. Deering Co., of Portland, be informed that the schooner had lost both her anchors. Aside from that, the *Carroll A. Deering* seemed to be in excellent condition, sailing along at about five nautical miles.

But two days later, on January 31, someone discovered her stranded ashore only a few miles from the lightship. Her crew of twelve officers and men had tracelessly disappeared. Officials from Diamond Shoals who boarded the vessel found evidence indicating that the crew had quickly abandoned ship—but for no apparent reason. The sails were set and the cargo intact, but the dory and motor lifeboat, along with most of the clothing, supplies, and provisions aboard, were gone.

After a hunt that took seventy days, the Coast Guard found not a trace of the crew, nor any wreckage from her boats. Because of a message found in a bottle by Christopher C. Ray on April 11, 1921, at Buxton Beach, North Carolina, an investigation of the disappearance of the crew of the *Carroll A. Deering* was launched by five branches of the federal government: the departments of State, Treasury, Navy, Commerce, and Justice.

The message? An unsigned note believed to have been written by the *Deering*'s mate, Engineer Henry Bates: "*Deering* captured by . . . something like a chaser, taking off everything. . . . Crew hiding all over ship. No chance to make escape. Finder please notify headquarters of Deering."

If the terrified crewmen were removed by a larger vessel, why were the lifeboats removed?

Such things have been occurring all over the world and are too numerous to be mere figments of the human imagination. They're real enough, but unless we postulate some unknown property of natural laws, there's no rational way to explain them.

It's a self-evident fact that nothing can exist—no object or condition—unless the laws of the universe allow it. It follows, therefore, that there is some undiscovered cause behind the strange disappearances of ships, planes, and people. It also follows that man's psychic potential, his intelligence, capacity for hostility, love, aggression, and fear are conscious elements of creation. The human mind and its emotions, because they exist, are as much a *deliberate* part of the universe as is the human body and brain.

Both individually and collectively, human thoughts and feelings are influenced by the environment—cosmic and terrestrial. Conversely, it's also true that "intangible" emotions and thoughts have a profound effect on this environment.

So struck was British scientist James Lovelock by the beauty of satellite photographs of the Earthly environment that he derived a fantastic theory about it. The Earth's blue atmosphere, he said, "is part of a living organism ... like the shell of a snail."

Rather than assuming that the Earth's environment conditions all life and determines which species survive and which perish, Lovelock inverted this concept and came up with the "Gaia hypothesis," named after the Earth goddess of the ancient Greeks. Instead of adapting to the planetary environment, said Lovelock, all life forms *shape and control it* in order to ensure their survival!

This was pretty heady stuff for a fifty-six-year-old Fellow of the Royal Society, but he had marshaled enough facts to support his strange contention. "It appears to me that the biosphere (all forms of terrestrial life combined) was able to *control* (psychically) the temperature of the Earth's surface and the composition of the atmosphere.... Living matter, the air, the oceans, and the land, all are parts of a gigantic system—'Gaia'—which behaves like a single organism—*even a living creature.*"

Not exactly a new idea, but revolutionary enough for our times. Old Ben Franklin believed and taught that the Earth was a living entity, as were all the other planets. He admonished his listeners to "pray only to your local diety, the Sun." Life couldn't exist anywhere in the solar system without the dynamic presence of our local star; life (as we know it) couldn't exist on Earth without its sustaining atmospheric blanket, oceanic waters—and *gravitational field.*

We know very little about the geomagnetic and gravitational field of our world. There seem to be places where—for a complex of reasons—the psychic and gravitational energies combine to form a vortex of teleportation. In 1899, near Baltic and Florida avenues in Atlantic City, New Jersey, according to dozens of eyewitness reports, a man was seen to sail skyward, legs and arms flailing. All the helpless watchers could do was gaze and listen in horror as the man repeatedly screamed, "Put me down!"

And a few miles from Gallatin, Tennessee, on the brilliant, sunny afternoon of September 23, 1880, David Lang left his house and walked across a forty-acre pasture to inspect a pair of quarter horses. His two children, eleven-year-old Sarah and eight-year-old George, were playing with some wooden horses and wagons their father had brought back from Nashville. The family cook and servants were working inside the house.

"Hurry back, Dave," his wife called after him, "I want you to drive me into town before the stores close." Lang stopped by the fence, glanced at his pocket watch, and waved. "I'll be back in a few minutes."

As he crossed the field, he waved once more as a horse and buggy carrying two friends, Judge August Peck and his brother-in-law, clattered up the long lane toward the house. The eyes of all five people were watching David Lang when he disappeared into thin air, never to return.

Mrs. Lang screamed in fear and horror; the children were shocked into incomprehending silence. Judge Peck and his brother-in-law scrambled from the buggy and raced across the field, followed by Mrs. Lang and the children. They examined the terrain carefully—over and over; there wasn't a bush or tree, a gully or hole to indicate how the man could have disappeared.

When the grief-stricken Mrs. Lang became hysterical, she was led, still screaming, into the house. One of the servants began to ring a huge bell in the side yard; alerted neighbors quickly began to arrive. As the sun went down, scores of people with lanterns searched every square inch of the field in which Lang had last been seen. They stomped and poked in hope of finding some hole into which he might have fallen.

All in vain. One second, David Lang was there; the next instant, he was gone. In subsequent weeks of follow-up examination, each of the witnesses to the bizarre event revealed that they'd all seen the same thing happen at the same time and place, yet none of them had been affected. A county surveyor probed the exact spot where Lang had vanished, and reported that it was solidly supported by a thick layer of limestone. There were no holes or caves.

Mrs. Lang lived a long time afterward, hoping, somehow, that her husband would return. He never did.

A number of months later, on a warm evening in 1881, Lang's two children noticed that at the spot where their father had last been seen there was a fifteen-foot circle of stunted, yellowish grass. Later, as they stood beside the circle, Sarah called out to her father. The youngsters reportedly heard his voice faintly—repeatedly calling for help—then the voice faded and was heard no more.

"I have many data of human disappearances," wrote Charles Fort in his book *New Lands*. "I also have data upon the fall of organic matter from the sky. Because of my familiarity with many records, it seems no more incredible that up in the seemingly unoccupied sky there should be hosts of living things than the seemingly blank of the ocean should swarm with life. I have many notes upon a phosphorescence, or electric or magnetic condition of things that fall from the sky. . . ."

Most of the known instances of disappearances are of solitary individuals, except in those cases where ships have been found adrift on the open sea, with coffee still hot in the galley's urn, uneaten plates of food on the tables, but no trace of officers or crew, and no clue as to what might have happened to them.

The selectivity of the force—or entity—is downright terrifying.

Seldom, however, are there reports of twenty or thirty people vanishing from some point on *land*. But that's just what happened on a raw November day in 1930 when trapper Joe Labelle approached a friendly Eskimo village about five hundred miles north of the Royal Canadian Mounties' base at Churchill. An icy wind was blowing off Lake Anjikuni, flapping the animal hides that were strung over the open doors of the Eskimo dwellings. He'd been friendly with the villagers for many years and had made a miles-wide detour across the icy tundra just to pay a short visit with his native friends.

An ominous silence swallowed up his first shouted greeting. He stopped and yelled again as he got closer. Still no answer. Joe drove his dog team up to the nearest hut, pushed aside a flap of caribou skin, and called inside.

It was empty. So was every tent dwelling in the whole village. It was absolutely incredible that there wouldn't be a single man, woman, or child left to guard the Eskimo homes in that forbidding area. He found full pots of food hanging over the remains of fires that had been cold for months. As in the galleys of abandoned ships, food had been set out to be eaten, but had never been touched. Joe wandered around the ominously empty village in a state of amazement, searching for some clue as to what had happened to the missing villagers. He found some sealskin clothing in a hut with the ivory needle still sticking in a child's garment where one of the mothers had abruptly stopped her mending job—because of what?

There wasn't a hint of an answer to any of the many mysteries that presented themselves. Several battered kayaks lay around on the beach, one of which he recognized as belonging to the village's headman. They had obviously been long abandoned, beaten into uselessness by the elements. But the most baffling mystery of all was the fact that the most prized possessions of the Eskimos—their rifles—leaned forlornly against the doorways of the empty huts and tents.

As the investigating Mounties quickly surmised (after Joe filed his report), no Eskimo with his wits about him would dream of taking a long trip without his rifle, which in the Far North can mean the difference between life and death. Yet here were all the abandoned guns! What had happened to these men? And where were their large, powerful dogs, which were as important in the northern wasteland as their rifles, if not more so?

When the Mounties arrived, they found that seven of the large canines had been tied to the stumps of some scrubby trees and had died—as was later determined—of starvation. Pathologists and other experts the Mounties had summoned spent two weeks at the site examining every scrap of evidence they could find. Because of the condition of certain kinds of berries found in the cooking pots, they deduced that by the time Joe Labelle found the village deserted, the Eskimos had been gone for about two months.

The mystery was exacerbated by the disappearance of a body from a grave fashioned by the Eskimos—a cairn of stones—on the side of the village opposite the bodies of the starved dogs. Grave robbing by Eskimos is unthinkable, but the stones removed from the cairn were stacked in two neat piles—a feat no animal could have accomplished. So who— or *what*—was responsible for the abrupt departure of the Eskimo villagers?

Whatever happened must have been totally unexpected, and virtually instantaneous. If indeed they had left their huts in the dead of early winter because of some overwhelming attraction, skilled trackers were totally unable to pick up a trail anywhere around the village. The battered kayaks bore mute testimony that they hadn't left by way of Lake Anjikuni. But they left—*or were taken*—so abruptly that they abandoned their dogs, guns, clothing, kayaks, and even the food on their fires. And there was also the plundered grave to consider.

Eight months of patient, painstaking investigation for hundreds of miles in all directions failed to turn up a single individual who had lived in the abandoned, now desolate village of Anjikuni.

The recent discovery of new subatomic particles ("psi" and "j") has led to the belief that a whole new series of such particles exists. One of these, tentatively called a "graviton," has triggered some of the most incredible scientific speculation in human history. Taking the existence of black holes (gravitationally collapsed stars so dense that nothing, not even light, can escape from them) as a model, scientists at particle-accelerator installations have postulated the existence of subatomic black holes—*i.e.*, tiny particles of such incredible density that they actually draw other material into themselves!

If submicroscopic black holes are ever proven to exist, they will radically alter our entire concept of the micro- *and* macro-cosmic universe. Such infinitesimally small gravitational anomalies could exist singly or in great multitudes, and if located underground, would have a pronounced effect on the abilities of dowsers. Before his death, John G. Shelley, of Lewiston, Maine (president of the American Society of Dowsers), said, "Although dowsing has no acceptable scientific explanation, I'm reasonably certain that some kind of rapport exists between the mind or thoughts of the dowser and the Earth's gravitational and electromagnetic field."

Ex-astronaut Edgar Mitchell, who successfully conducted a series of telepathic tests with psychic Olaf Jonsson while returning from the Moon, found that his psychic ability was enhanced by zero gravity. Another astronaut, James Irwin, also experienced strengthened telepathic phenomena while in the relatively weak gravitational field of the lunar surface. Olaf Jonsson, incidentally, has since used his remarkable talents in the area of the Bermuda Triangle to locate an eight-foot heavy gold chain valued at $200,000, and—in a previous astounding display of psychic power—guided professional divers to $300,000 worth of a treasure trove that had lain on the floor of the Atlantic Ocean since 1662. He is now on the trail of a fabulous $600-million fortune that sank with a Spanish treasure fleet about a hundred miles east of Key West, Florida.

When ships and aircraft disappear, even when there's no trace of wreckage or other debris, it's conceivable that they met with a perfectly natural disaster that caused the vessels to sink to the bottom of the Atlantic with all hands aboard. But when, as was the case of the *Carroll A. Deering* and other vessels, the ship is later found intact but *abandoned* . . . ?

The *Mary Celeste* was a case in point. She was found drifting on the afternoon of December 5, 1872, by the skipper of a British brigantine—out of New York, sailing between the Azores and Portugal—en route to Gibraltar. Captain Morehouse of the *Dei Gratia* dispatched three sailors to board the drifting *Mary Celeste* to render assistance. Totally baffled, the men reported in about an hour that there wasn't a soul aboard; the entire ship's company—including a cat—had vanished. Her compass was broken, all hatches were wide open, all lifeboats were gone, and the wheel unmanned, turning freely. The ship's navigation book, sextant, and chronometer were gone. The galley was found to be neat and tidy, and a cargo of almost two thousand barrels of alcohol was found intact in the hold.

The personal effects of the crew were also found intact. None of the sailors' personal belongings had been touched. In the skipper's cabin, searchers found his books, raincoat, and pipe on the floor next to his bunk. The sailors' lockers contained considerable sums of money and various other valuables. According to the last entry in the ship's log (found in the mate's cabin), the *Mary Celeste* had passed within six miles of the island of Santa Marie in the Azores at eight o'clock in the morning.

For some mysterious reason, she had been hastily (perhaps forcibly) abandoned by all hands sometime between 8:00 A.M. and noon.

More recently—on February 3, 1940—the *Gloria Colite*, a 125-foot schooner out of Saint Vincent, British West Indies, was sighted by the U.S. Coast Guard cutter *Cardigan* about 150 miles south of Mobile, Alabama. Captain and crew had inexplicably disappeared, leaving the *Gloria Colite* drifting aimlessly. Her foresails were set, but badly ripped; her mainsail, steering, and rigging were gone, and her deck housing was wrecked. The *Cardigan* took the derelict in tow to Mobile, where a full investigation was made—unsuccessfully, as it turned out.

On October 22, 1944, a ninety-ton Cuban cargo ship, the *Rubicon*, was spotted—apparently abandoned—by a Navy blimp in the Gulf Stream about forty miles southeast of Key Largo. The dirigible notified the Coast Guard, which dispatched two ships to investigate. When the Coast Guard arrived, they found the derelict *Rubicon* being towed by an American banana boat. All four vessels proceeded to Miami, where they put into the quarantine dock.

In the investigation that followed, the Navy found that the last entry in the ship's log was almost a month previously, on September 26, when she had put into Havana—only about two hundred miles from where the abandoned *Rubicon* was discovered. The only living thing aboard her was a half-starved dog. Not even a wild guess was made as to the disappearance of the captain and crew of the *Rubicon*.

And so it went—and still goes. Chances are that the now famous incident of the disappearance of five TBM Avenger torpedo bombers on December 5, 1945 (out of Fort Lauderdale Naval Air Station in Florida), was preceded by the disappearance of the pilots from their cockpits. The flying boat and *its* crew also disappeared into the limbo of lost planes, men, and ships.

Human thought and emotion are affected by variations in the gravitational field, and so may be physical *objects*. It has been speculated that the most powerful gravity wells in the universe—the black holes—may be supercolossal avenues into another part of the universe or another dimension.

Something very much like them—*on a much smaller scale*—could exist within our planetary system, even right here on Earth. They may be perfectly natural phenomena but totally beyond our present scientific understanding.

Or ... they may be *artificial* fields used by intelligent beings for some unfathomable purpose.

(What does a tropical fish make of being scooped out of its aquarium?)

17. "An Imaginary Area..."

A U.S. Coast Guard statement

The U.S. Coast Guard is the government agency responsible for policing the high seas, and its investigations into the various mysterious disappearances of ships in the Bermuda Triangle area have formed the bases of much of the speculation on facts and causes of these disasters. But what does the Coast

Guard itself think about the background and validity of these reports and the various interpretations they have provoked? Following is the text of a memorandum circulated by the U.S. Coast Guard; only biographical references have been eliminated, as these duplicate entries in the Selected Bibliography to be found at the end of this volume.

THE "Bermuda or Devil's Triangle" is an imaginary area located off the southeastern Atlantic coast of the United States, which is noted for a high incidence of unexplained losses of ships, small boats, and aircraft. The apexes of the triangle are generally accepted to be Bermuda, Miami, Florida, and San Juan, Puerto Rico.

In the past, extensive, but futile Coast Guard searches prompted by search and rescue cases such as the disappearances of an entire squadron of TBM Avengers shortly after take off from Fort Lauderdale, Florida, or the traceless sinking of the *Marine Sulphur Queen* in the Florida Straits have lent credence to the popular belief in the mystery and the supernatural qualities of the "Bermuda Triangle."

Countless theories attempting to explain the many disappearances have been offered throughout the history of the area. The most practical seem to be environmental and those citing human error.

The majority of disappearances can be attributed to the area's unique environmental features. First, the "Devil's Triangle" is one of the two places on earth that a magnetic compass does point toward true north. Normally it points toward magnetic north. The difference between the two is known as compass variation. The amount of variation changes by as much as twenty degrees as one circumnavigates the earth. If this compass variation or error is not compensated for, a navigator could find himself far off course and in deep trouble.

An area called the "Devil's Sea" by Japanese and Filipino seamen, located off the east coast of Japan, also exhibits the same magnetic characteristics. As the "Bermuda Triangle" it is known for its mysterious disappearances.

Another environmental factor is the character of the Gulf Stream. It is extremely swift and turbulent and can quickly erase any evidence of a disaster. The unpredictable Caribbean-Atlantic weather pattern also plays its role. Sudden local thunder storms and water spouts often spell disaster for pilots and mariners. And finally, the topography of the ocean floor varies from extensive shoals around the islands to some of the deepest marine trenches in the world. With the interaction of the strong currents over the many reefs the topography is in a state of constant flux and development of new navigational hazards is swift.

Not to be under estimated is the human error factor. A large number of pleasure boats travel the waters between Florida's Gold Coast and the Bahamas. All too often, crossings are attempted with too small a boat, insufficient knowledge of the area's hazards, and a lack of good seamanship.

The Coast Guard, in short, is not impressed with supernatural explanations of disasters at sea. It has been our experience that the combined forces of nature and unpredictability of mankind outdo even the most far fetched science fiction many times each year.

18. Bermuda Triangle Victims

compiled by Vincent H. Gaddis

Disappearing ships and aircraft, vessels with vanished crews. Beginning with the year 1800, here is a list of these victims. No list, of course, could be complete, but this one, comprising the more prominent incidents, was made after a survey of available literature on the subject.

1800 The USS *Pickering*, en route to Guadeloupe, West Indies, from New Castle, Delaware, disappeared with its crew of ninety men.

1814 The USS *Wasp*, with 140 sailors, was last heard from in the Caribbean on October 9.

1824 The USS *Wild Cat* vanished on October 28 while en route to Thompson's Island from Cuba with a crew of fourteen.

1840 The *Rosalie*, a French ship bound for Havana, was discovered in shipshape condition but abandoned. The only living thing aboard was a half-starved canary in a cage.

1843 The USS *Grampus* was Charleston-bound when she was sighted off Saint Augustine, Florida, on March 3. She was never seen again.

1854 Although in excellent condition, the schooner *Bella* was found crewless in the West Indies.

1855 Evidence of a hasty abandonment was found aboard the *James B. Chester* when it was discovered some six hundred miles southwest of the Azores. Every boat was still hanging in the davits. Provisions and the cargo were intact.

1880 The British frigate HMS *Atalanta*, a training ship with more than two hundred cadets and sailors aboard, left Bermuda for England and vanished.

1881 A deserted schooner was found west of the Azores by the brig *Ellen Austin*. Everything aboard was shipshape, but her log and trail boards were missing. A prize crew was put aboard for salvage. The two ships were separated in a storm, and when they were rejoined, the salvage crew had disappeared. Another crew was placed aboard. Again the vessels became separated, and the mystery ship was never seen again.

1902 On October 3 the German bark *Freya* set sail for Chile from Cuba. Twenty days later she was found partly dismasted, with nobody aboard. Weather reports showed there had been only light winds in the region.

1909 Joshua Slocum, in 1895–1898, became the first man to complete a solo trip around the world. He made the 46,000-mile voyage in his thirty-six-foot yawl, the *Spray*. On November 19, 1909, he sailed from Miami in the *Spray* for a solo cruise through the West Indies. Slocum and his famed yawl were never heard from again.

1910 On March 15, the Navy tug USS *Nina* departed from the Norfolk Navy Yard for Havana. She was seen off Savannah, Georgia, steaming south. Then she disappeared forever.

1918 The USS *Cyclops*, a Navy coal ship, sailed from Barbados for Baltimore on March 4. Considered one of the Navy's most baffling mysteries, the huge vessel vanished with 308 men, including Consul General Alfred L. M. Gottschalk.

1921 Mysteriously deserted, on January 31 the five-masted schooner *Carroll A. Deering* ran aground at Cape Hatteras, North Carolina. The only life aboard were two cats.

1921 During the first half of this year so many vessels vanished that five departments of the government were investigating. All of these vessels had sailed from a port on the East Coast of the United States. Some had entered the Triangle area; others skirted around to the north of it. Among the larger ships mysteriously missing were the Italian steamer *Monte San Michele*, the British steamer *Esperanza de Larrinaga*, the Brazilian ship *Cabedello*, the British tanker *Ottawa*, the sulphur transport *Hewitt*, as well as smaller vessels like the Norwegian barks *Svartskog*, the *Steinsund*, and the *Florino*. There is no knowledge at all of the fate of these vessels. Several months earlier two other ships sailed from the East Coast into the unknown. They were the Spanish steamer *Yute* and the Russian bark *Albyan*.

1925 "Danger like dagger now. Come quick!" That was the last radio message from the Japanese freighter *Raifuku Maru* from a location near the Bahama Islands. It has been suggested that the "dagger" may have been a waterspout, but no wreckage or bodies were found.

1925 The SS *Cotopaxi*, a large cargo ship, sailed from Charleston for Havana and vanished.

1926 Sailing south from Port Newark, the freighter *Suduffco* entered the limbo of the lost with its crew of twenty-nine men.

1931 With forty-three persons aboard, the freighter *Stavanger* was last located south of Cat Island in the Bahamas.

1938 In March the *Anglo-Australian* with a crew of thirty-nine vanished somewhere southwest of the Azores.

1940 In February the U.S. Coast Guard found the yacht *Gloria Colite*, of Saint Vincent, British West Indies, two hundred miles south of Mobile, Alabama, deserted. Everything was in order. Seas were calm. There was "no indication as to the cause of the abandonment."

1941 Two sister ships sailing from the same port of Saint Thomas, Virgin Islands, for Norfolk with cargoes of bauxite vanished only seventeen days apart. The *Proteus* sailed on November 23, and the *Nereus* on December 10.

1941 An SOS came from the freighter *Mahukona*, located six hundred miles east of Jacksonville, Florida: "Lowering boats ... crew abandoning ship." Four vessels sped toward the stricken vessel. No wreckage was sighted, nor could any survivors be found.

1944 The Cuban freighter *Rubicon* was sighted drifting off Florida's east coast by a Navy blimp. When a Coast Guard cutter from Miami arrived, the crew found the only living thing aboard was a dog. A lifeboat was missing, and a broken hawser was hanging down from the bow.

1945 On December 5 Flight 19, consisting of five TBM Avenger torpedo bombers, left the Naval Air Station at Fort Lauderdale, Florida, on a routine patrol flight east of Florida. Radio messages midway during the flight revealed that the pilots were lost, that every gyro and compass in all planes was "going crazy," and that they couldn't tell which direction was west. They estimated their position as about 225 miles northeast of the station. The final message from the lost patrol ended in mid-sentence. A Martin Mariner flying boat patrol plane with a crew of thirteen men was sent to the rescue. All five bombers as well as the rescue plane were never heard from again. Despite a 380,000-square-mile search, no wreckage, oil slicks, or bodies were found.

1945 On December 27 it was reported that two large schooners were overdue. One was the seventy-foot *Voyager II*, being taken down the intercoastal waterway by a retired Army officer sailing with his three teen-age children. The other was the two-masted *Valmore*, with a crew of four, off the North Carolina coast. Neither vessel was ever found.

1946 The *City Belle*, a 120-foot two-masted schooner, en route from the Dominican Republic to Nassau stopped at Turks Islands to unload part of its cargo of lumber and to take on twenty-two passengers on December 2. Three days later it was discovered completely deserted about three hundred miles southeast of Miami. The passengers' personal effects were still aboard. Only the lifeboats were missing. An extensive search for the boats was futile.

1947 An American Army C-54 Superfortress was lost about one hundred miles from Bermuda.

1948 On January 30 the *Star Tiger*, a huge four-engined Tudor IV owned by British-South American Airways, radioed the control tower at Bermuda that it was four hundred miles to the northeast. Then it vanished with its twenty-five passengers and crew of six. The pilot had reported weather conditions excellent. Nothing was found despite a widespread search.

1948 Al Snyder, internationally famous jockey, and two friends left Miami on March 5 to go fishing near Sandy Key. They anchored their cabin cruiser and left in a skiff to fish in the nearby shallow waters. They never returned. A search by more than a thousand men, a hundred boats, and fifty planes got under way. The skiff was found beside a small unnamed island near Rabbit Key, sixty miles north of the cabin cruiser. A $15,000 reward for a rescue of the men or recovery of their bodies was never claimed.

1948 A DC-3 airliner chartered for a predawn flight from Puerto Rico to Miami carried thirty-two passengers and a crew of three. It was December 28, and the passengers had been spending the Christmas holidays on the island. Fifty miles out, with the lights of Miami aglow in the night sky ahead, the captain sent his last message that all was well and he was standing by for landing instructions. He never arrived. Again, no wreckage or bodies.

1949 On January 17 the *Star Ariel,* sister ship to the *Star Tiger* that vanished a year previously, was on the four-hour, one-thousand-mile hop between Bermuda and Jamaica when the veteran captain reported fair weather. Then the airliner vanished into the thin air through which it flew. A vast air and surface search by the U.S. Navy, then on maneuvers south of Bermuda, was all in vain.

1949 While the search for the *Star Ariel* was continuing, a fishing boat, the *Driftwood,* disappeared on a trip between Fort Lauderdale and Bimini with five men aboard.

1950 An American Globemaster disappeared in March on a flight to Ireland.

1950 The SS *Sandra,* a 350-foot freighter, sailed from Savannah, Georgia, for Venezuela in June. She passed Jacksonville and Saint Augustine along the well-traveled coastal shipping lane in calm weather, then disappeared without leaving a trace.

1950 During this same month of June, a DC-3 owned by the New Tribes Mission of Chico, California, took off from Miami for Venezuela with ten missionaries and five children. A fuel stop was made at Kingston, and it then left for Maracaibo. Instead it flew into the limbo of the lost.

1951 Destined for scrapping, the *São Paulo,* carrying a caretaker crew of eight, was being towed by two seagoing tugs the night of October 3–4 southwest of the Azores. Because of rough seas, one of the tugs released its lines. With morning dawn the *São Paulo* had disappeared, leaving the cables on the second tug broken. It, too, had entered the bourn of lost ships.

1953 A British York transport, with thirty-three passengers and a crew of six, vanished on a flight to Jamaica. In this case an SOS was sent, which ended abruptly without explanation or giving the aircraft's position.

1954 A U.S. Navy Super Constellation disappeared north of the Triangle area. There were forty-two people aboard, some of them wives and children. Although the huge aircraft carried two transmitters, no radio signals were received.

1954 The *Southern Districts*, a bulk carrier tanker, was en route from Port Sulphur, Texas, to Bucksport, Maine, when she disappeared in December. A converted Navy LST, she was 328 feet long and carried a crew of twenty-three.

1955 In January the sixty-five-foot schooner *Home Sweet Home* sailed from Bermuda for Antigua across the Sargasso Sea. It vanished with seven persons aboard in the one-time "Graveyard of Lost Ships."

1955 The yacht *Connemara IV*, of New York registry, was found crewless and adrift four hundred miles southwest of Bermuda in September.

1956 On April 5 a B-25 converted to a civilian cargo plane was lost southeast of Tongue of the Ocean with three persons aboard.

1956 A Navy Martin patrol seaplane P5M vanished with a crew of ten near Bermuda on November 9. No radio signals were received.

1958 On New Year's Day the racing yacht *Revonoc* owned by publisher Harvey Conover, an expert seaman, vanished on a trip between Key West and Miami, a route in which they were always in sight of land.

1962 A huge Air Force KB-50 tanker left Langley Air Force Base, Virginia, on January 8 on a fueling operation. A distorted distress signal was picked up by the tower a short time later. Within minutes a search was under way, but no trace of the aircraft or the eight men aboard was ever found.

1963 With a crew of thirty-nine, the *Marine Sulphur Queen* began its final voyage on February 2 from Beaumont, Texas, for Norfolk. A radio message two nights later placed the vessel near the Dry Tortugas. When it was overdue, a search was launched. Some debris and a life jacket believed to be from the tanker were found fourteen miles southeast of Key West.

1963 Although some debris was recovered, the sixty-three-foot fishing boat *Sno' Boy* has been listed as a Triangle victim. It left Kingston on July 2 for Northeast Cay, eighty miles southeast of Jamaica, with forty persons aboard.

1963 Two new Air Force KC-135 four-engine Stratotanker jets left Homestead Air Force Base, south of Miami, to classified refueling range in the Atlantic. The crews totaled eleven men. Weather good. Their last radio message before vanishing placed them three hundred miles southwest of Bermuda.

1963 A C-132 Cargomaster disappeared on September 22 while en route to the Azores.

1965 A C-119 Air Force Reserve cargo plane with ten men aboard left Homestead Air Force Base on June 5 for Grand Turk Island. An extensive search ended with a Coast Guard report: "Results negative. There are no conjectures."

1965 George Boston was the first Harvard freshman football player to score a touchdown against Yale. On October 28, while delivering the *El Gato*, a forty-five-foot catamaran-type houseboat to a buyer in Puerto Rico, he disappeared somewhere between Great Inagua and Grand Turk islands.

1967 With four men aboard, a Chase YC-122, converted to a cargo plane, vanished between Palm Beach and Grand Bahama on January 11.

1967 Robert Van Westerborg, a Miami business consultant, and Phillip de Berard, Jr., Southern Bell Telephone Company executive, with their wives, took off from Key Largo to photograph the site of a new microwave relay station. The aircraft and all four aboard were never seen again. The date was January 14.

1967 Phillip Quigley disappeared in his light plane on January 11 on a flight from Cozumel to Honduras.

1967 A twin-engine Piper Apache on a chartered flight between San Juan and Saint Thomas vanished on January 18. Lost were Stephan R. Currier, noted philanthropist, and his wife, the daughter of David Bruce, the U.S. ambassador to Great Britain and heir to seven hundred million dollars.

1967 James Horton and Charles Griggs, two Florida doctors, disappeared on a flight between Jamaica and Nassau on

March 23. An urgent distress message was picked up by a military plane—then silence.

1967 In October Mr. and Mrs. Hector Guzmán, of Puerto Rico, were returning home from Fort Lauderdale. They refueled their twin-engine plane at Great Inagua Island and took off into the unknown.

1967 Dan Burrack, a Miami Beach hotel owner, with two friends, took his cabin cruiser, the *Witchcraft*, out to buoy number 7 on December 22 to see the Christmas lights of Miami a mile from shore. At 9:00 P.M. the Coast Guard received a radio message from Burrack that his boat had become disabled after the propellers of his outdrivers had struck a submerged object. He said he was in no danger. Eighteen minutes later a Coast Guard vessel arrived at the buoy. Only the buoy was there; there was no sign of the disabled craft or its occupants.

1968 The *Ithaca Island*, a freighter, vanished on a voyage from Norfolk to Liverpool.

1969 On June 6 Caroline Coscio, a Miami Beach nurse, and a male companion left Pompano Beach, Florida, for a flight to Jamaica. After a refueling stop at Georgetown, she headed for Grand Turk Island. At 7:35 P.M. the tower operator at Grand Turk received a message that her directional equipment was not working and she was lost. She said she was over two small islands, but "there was nothing down there." At this time, guests at the Ambergris Cay Hotel were watching her plane circling. She flew off, and her final message at 8:22 P.M. was, "I'm out of fuel! I'm going down!"

1969 Within a twelve-day period, between June 30 and July 10, five deserted vessels were found drifting in the same general area of the Atlantic Ocean. The *Vagabond*, a twenty-foot sloop found by the Swedish ship *Golar Frost*. The British steamer *Cotopaxi* found a yacht headed east on automatic steering, but not a soul aboard. The *Maplebank* discovered a sixty-foot vessel floating keel-up. The *Picardy* found the *Teignmouth Electron*. A sixty-nine-foot vessel, also floating bottom-up, was found by the British tanker *Helisoma*.

1969 On November 4 the yacht *Southern Cross* was found mysteriously abandoned off Cape May, New Jersey.

1970 The *Milton Iatrides*, a freighter, vanished while en route from New Orleans to Cape Town.

1971 On April 3 the freighter *Elizabeth* set sail from Port Everglades for Venezuela with a cargo of paper. Two days later she radioed her position as in the Windward Passage between Haiti and Cuba. Then she vanished.

1971 An F-4 Phantom II jet fighter left Homestead Air Force Base on September 10. A radar check followed the plane's position to a point eighty-five miles southeast of Miami. Then the "blip" disappeared. An immediate but futile search was made in this area, where the water is no more than thirty feet deep.

1971 The 338-foot motor ship *Caribe* set sail from Colombia for the Dominican Republic on October 9 with a crew of twenty-eight men. Her final radio message placed her at about halfway on her voyage. No distress signal was ever received.

1971 The *Lucky Edur*, a twenty-five-foot radio-equipped fishing vessel, was found deserted on October 31 off the New Jersey coast by the Coast Guard. The weather was excellent. All ten life preservers were aboard.

1972 On October 21 a Flamingo Airlines plane departed from Bimini and vanished without a trace.

1973 The *Anita*, a 20,000-ton freighter with a crew of thirty-two, sailed from Norfolk into the unknown on March 21.

1974 The fifty-four-foot yacht *Saba Bank* left Nassau March 10 on a shakedown cruise to Miami. A futile search for her by the Coast Guard was suspended on April 27.

19. Our Fascination with Disaster

by Martin Ebon

Why is there a nationwide, and even worldwide, fascination with disasters or threats of disasters? Over the years, self-styled prophets have proclaimed everything from a firm date for the disintegration of southern California to the "end of the world." As Mr. Ebon sees it, there exists an underlying pyschological fascination with panic and terror, with threats from irresistible supernatural powers, and with the existence of unknown forces. Martin Ebon, editor of this volume, served for twelve years as administrative secretary of the Parapsychology Foundation and has edited a variety of peri-

133

odicals and books in the field of extrasensory perception and the occult. Among his works are Prophecy in Our Time, They Knew the Unknown, *and* The Devil's Bride: Exorcism, Past and Present.

LET'S face it: there is virtually no chance of proving or disproving the basic phenomenon of the Bermuda Triangle with present-day scientific techniques. It may be possible to find concrete explanations for one or another of the mysterious disappearances, or, on the other hand, to discover in the end that it is inexplicable—but we will never, with current methods, get to the bottom of the pattern governing them all.

The pattern itself is, of course, in dispute. Vincent Gaddis, who now regrets that he ever used the "triangle" label, notes that the disappearances have taken place within a much less easily defined area. And Ivan Sanderson, who spoke of lozenge-shaped areas in many parts of the world, also admitted that it was difficult to fit them into any precise geometric shape.

So, now we know that we are not really dealing with disasters that took place within a precisely defined area, but with clusters of events that defy exact geometric labels.

Next, let us be fully aware that these disappearances of planes, ships, and people occurred over a relatively long period of time. As a result, the records available to us are far from uniform in quality. The USS *Cyclops* disappeared during World War I, the Avenger planes during World War II. Other disappearances took place before, after, and between the two wars. Human testimony is subject to distortion, as any casual student of human psychology well knows; even the most routine car collision will result in widely differing descriptions as to how it happened and who was at fault.

In other words, we are dealing here with an odd assortment of events that have been called "mysterious" for a variety of reasons. Anything that can't be easily explained might be labeled mysterious, and there is hardly anyone among us who doesn't just love a mystery. If something can't be explained, or if the explanation is too prosaic, a conspiracy hypothesis often pleases people much more than the barren truth. That is why, more than a decade after the assassination of President John F. Kennedy, reports and rumors of a possible conspiracy connected with his murder continue to crop up.

In discussions about a conspiracy, there is usually a reference to the elusive "They," who are supposed to have planned coup, a murder, an economic crisis, a stock-market rise or drop, a war, or other disasters. There are enough real conspiracies or would-be conspiracies around to satisfy the avid student of connivance. But "They" are suspected in more dramatic events than an Arizona land swindle or a Florida condominium collapse. Some sort of "They" has been suspected behind every series of puzzling events during the past few decades, particularly the sightings of Unidentified Flying Objects (UFO's), also known as Flying Saucers.

In fact, the Bermuda Triangle fascination is quite similar to the excitement over UFO's. We have experienced public interest waves in related fields, such as the hypothesis that the earth was visited by "gods from outer space," who were said to have established much of our life pattern, beliefs, and technology. Hand-in-hand with inexplicable, awe-inspiring ideas of this sort has been the fascination among filmgoers with motion pictures on such subjects as devastating earthquakes, the sinking of giant ocean liners, and uncontrolled fires in skyscraper office buildings.

Where does all this fascination with disasters come from, since there seems to be trouble enough in the real world without having to add fictional, film-studio-designed mass mayhem, including stories and movies about invasions by millions of voracious insects or deadly microbes from outer space?

Reality, it seems, is never enough! We want more, and more, and more.

Remember the first landings on the moon? All of us were glued to our television sets, getting up around 4:00 A.M. to see the live transmissions of our astronauts landing on the moon and making their way across the lunar landscape. And now blasé we have become! Later moon landings seemed anticlimactic, and yesterday's astronaut heroes now make commercial promotion tours, reveal their emotional crises in autobiographies, or get quietly divorced.

These, we have discovered, are not supermen. Nor are our leaders in government, industry, religion, entertainment, and education any longer awe-inspiring or even trust-inspiring (if they ever were!), and we are in search of . . . of what?

We are in search of gods.

We are in search of beings more powerful and wiser than we are. We are in search of reassurance and, barring that, in search of fear and awe. If supernatural beings snatch planes out of the sky, pick up or pull down ships, then these are creatures more powerful than ourselves. They are godlike

135

beings. Perhaps they are so powerful and so knowledgeable that they know the answers to questions we are unable to answer. Because, here we are, coming to the end of the twentieth century, and we feel as if we were the most bewildered lot of human beings the earth has ever known.

And so we find patterns in awesome things, or just inexplicable or coincidental things. Sanderson is right when he sees a pattern in disappearances and seeks to sort them out. And Lawrence Kubsche is right when he finds that much of the speculation about the Bermuda Triangle is little more than a house of cards, with one thin bit of evidence piled upon another.

All this didn't happen yesterday afternoon. We didn't invent a pattern of thought that made fascination with UFO's, gods from outer space, or disappearances in a nautical triangle the content of mass attraction. The British philosopher David Hume (1711–1776) wrote in his *Essays* that "Prodigies, omens, oracles, judgements quite obscure the few natural events that are intermingled with them." He refers to "the usual propensity of mankind toward the marvellous," which may now and then be less prominent, but "can never be thoroughly extirpated from human nature."

Professor Gustav Jahoda, of the University of Strathclyde, Glasgow, Scotland, notes in his book *The Psychology of Superstition* that psychological surveys have shown certain types of personalities particularly prone to superstitious beliefs, notably the feeling that "one's fate is in the hands of unknown external powers, governed by forces over which one has no control." Science does not immunize against superstition. Scientific facts may be used to bolster superstitious thinking—just as the existence of the Saint Andreas fault, running north to south in southern California, not only may support objective analyses that this area is more earthquake-prone than others, but also may prompt apocalyptic seers into forecasting specific dates for such a disaster (happily, these have, up to the time of this writing, proven to be false).

Times of stress make for fascination with the supernatural, and these are times of such rapid changes and uncertainties that even illusory certainties are being craved. We are forced to adjust our thought patterns, our moral and even financial values with such rapidity that we are a generation suffering, as has been aptly said, from "future shock." Small wonder that hints of supernatural forces, even if engaged in such inexplicable activities as snatching planes and boats from the

Caribbean without leaving any traces, attract our ambivalent fascination.

But are we really under more stress than generations and centuries preceding our own? Everyone thinks he is unique, and what the late Henry Luce once pronounced "The American Century" certainly has produced brand-new risks, challenges, and fears. And yet, the Dutch philosopher Baruch Spinoza (1632–1677) found in his own society that "men would never be superstitious, if they could govern all their circumstances by rules, or if they were always favored by fortune." However, he noted in his *Tractatus Theologico-Politicus* that we are "frequently driven into situations where all rules are useless, and being often kept fluctuating pitiably between hope and fear by the uncertainty of fortune's greedily coveted favors." Thus, Spinoza concluded, men are "for the most part very prone to credulity."

I think that the riddle of the Bermuda Triangle must be seen against the background of the religio-cultural crisis of our time. Once again, mankind is proceeding in search of gods, looking with desperation and hope to beings greater than man himself, and certainly more efficient in going about the business of running life on earth. It has become a truism that we have experienced a revival of occultism, because established religions have failed to meet the needs of current society. But that is only partly true. Religious Fundamentalism has shown remarkable strength in nearly all denominations at the present time. And, indeed, it is in the Bible that we find apocalyptic parallels to some of the scenes that have been suggested by accounts of the Bermuda Triangle disappearances. Saint John, in Revelation, describes a scene that bears a close resemblance to those implied during various ship and plane disasters in the area. John may have witnessed a submarine earthquake in the Aegean Sea while he was staying on the island of Patmos. The New English Bible quotes him as saying, ". . . and I saw a star that had fallen from heaven to earth, and the star was given the key of the shaft of the abyss. With this he opened the shaft of the abyss; and from the shaft smoke rose like the smoke from a great furnace, and the sun and the air were darkened, by the smoke from the shaft."

Revelation has always had a great attraction for painters and poets of apocalyptic themes. It is a work of epic power, of sin, suffering, disaster, and redemption; it is a work for all ages, including our own. It speaks to us at a time when we have become conscious of the dangers of ecological suicide,

137

wars prompted by starvation, and the overall risk of simply using up the earth's resources by overpopulation and greed.

And yet, what is it within us that asks either to be saved or to be destroyed by a Power Greater Than Ourselves?

Psychologists and psychotherapists, back to Sigmund Freud and C. G. Jung, have speculated that our childhood feelings for our parents, notably our fathers, are reflected in lifetime attitudes toward God, religion, and anything that is supernatural. The firm and fair "father figure" has become absent from our society. We no longer have kings or queens, not even the pseudo-royalty of Hollywood movie stars, or the Camelot atmosphere that existed in Washington during the "reign" of John and Jacqueline Kennedy. Instead, we have experienced a revulsion against leadership personalities or leadership pretenders on all levels of modern society, notably after the Watergate scandals during the administration of President Richard M. Nixon. Small wonder we look elsewhere for the firmness and fairness, the power and strength that seem to have evaporated from human society!

The disappearances in the Bermuda Triangle were of very material things: ships and planes. Of course, people were on these vehicles, but the accounts emphasize the sizes and types of boats, their capacities, routes, and technical performance. It is a significant emphasis, because it implies that the disappearance of something as prosaic as a sulphur-carrying vessel is somehow more convincing than that of the people on it. There is an illusion of material certainty about the wingspread of a plane, the generator performance of a ship; it is all very technological, modern, and therefore a no-nonsense type of supernaturalism.

Dr. Harold F. Searles, a Washington, D.C., psychiatrist of extensive practical experience, has noted in his book *The Nonhuman Environment* that we tend to make inanimate objects into vehicles of our own emotions. I think that one of the most traumatic experiences of U.S. society in the 1970's was the end of its love affair with the automobile, finding it reduced from a glamorous partner and object of lavish attention to a gas-guzzling dependent. At any rate, Dr. Searles sees nonhuman elements among the "most basically important ingredients of human experience." He writes that "there is within the human individual a sense, whether at a conscious or unconscious level, of relatedness to his nonhuman environment, that this relatedness is one of the transcendentally important facts of human living."

Is it, then, too much to assume that the lost ships and

planes of the Bermuda Triangle gained so much attention in our time because they were extensions of ourselves, symbols of our own role as helpless and confused creatures, at the mercy of vast unknown forces, either friendly, or hostile, or neutral?

I think that is precisely what has happened. The evidence for actual supernatural forces working within the Bermuda Triangle is slender and fragmentary. The evidence for the impact of its underlying concept on ourselves is tremendous. The search for new gods began before man was capable of setting down his thoughts on cuneiform tablets, on papyrus, in the written and the printed word. Our technology has speeded it up. The pace is hectic, the field wide open. Fundamentalists, gurus, mind-control advocates, astrologers, seers of all types, spokesmen of New Religions, of a New Paganism, and of a rigid adherence to Scripture, are in competition for our minds and, presumably, our souls.

We are really looking for certainties that do not exist; and if they do exist, our minds and our senses are probably insufficiently equipped to recognize them. Civilizations beneath the sea may be defending their own ecology against our Caribbean and Atlantic shipping. Unidentified flying objects may be snatching planes out of the air for laboratory studies you and I cannot possibly imagine. Impersonal magnetic forces may be playing havoc with our known physical laws. But the only thing we can be sure of is our own fascination and, to a degree, the reasons for it. Beyond that, let us be guided by the great twelfth-century philosopher Moses Maimonides, who wrote, 'Teach thy tongue to say, 'I do not know.' "

IV

APPENDIX

TREASURY DEPARTMENT
UNITED STATES COAST GUARD

COMMANDANT
U.S. COAST GUARD
HEADQUARTERS
WASHINGTON 25, D.C.

•MVI-3
5943/MARINE SULPHUR
QUEEN o-8 Bd
1 7 MAR 1964

Commandant's Action

on

Marine Board of Investigation; disappearance of
the SS MARINE SULPHUR QUEEN at sea on or about
4 February 1963 with the presumed loss of all
persons on board

1. The record of the Marine Board of Investigation convened to investigate subject casualty together with the findings of fact, conclusions and recommendations has been reviewed.

2. The SS MARINE SULPHUR QUEEN, a T2-SE-A1 type tank vessel of U. S. Registry, converted to carry molten sulphur, departed Beaumont, Texas, with a full cargo of 15,260 tons on the afternoon of 2 February 1963 enroute Norfolk, Va. The ship and crew of 39 men disappeared. The vessel was last heard from at 0125 EST on 4 February 1963.

3. The ship's conversion in 1960 to a molten sulphur carrier necessitated the removal of all transverse bulkheads in way of the original centerline, tanks and modification of the internal structure to accommodate one continuous independent tank 306 ft. long, 30 ft. 6 in. wide and 33 ft. high, which was internally divided by transverse bulkheads into four cargo tanks of about equal size. The external surfaces of this long independent tank were insulated with a fibrous glass material 6" thick on the top of the tank and 4 in. thick on other surfaces. A void surrounded the tank which allowed a space about 3 ft. 6 in. between the bottom of the tank and the bottom plating of the ship, 2 ft. between the sides of the tank and the original wing tank longitudinal bulkheads, and 3 ft. between the top of the tank and the weather deck. A watertight bulkhead was installed at frame 59 which divided the void into two spaces. The forward space contained cargo tanks one and two and the after space contained cargo tanks three and four. A partial or diaphragm bulkhead which did not extend to the top or bottom of the void was installed where the first and second cargo tanks were divided at frame 65 and where the third and fourth cargo tanks were divided at frame 53. Near its midpoint the tank was welded to its supporting structures at frame 59, and provision was made to permit

Reproduced above is the first sheet of the summary of the findings of the Marine Board of Investigations, as reviewed by Admiral E. J. Roland, Commandant, U.S. Coast Guard Headquarters, Washington, D.C., together with the Commandant's comments on safeguards and procedures that might help to avoid other marine disasters of this type.

20. Disappearance of
the SS *Marine Sulphur Queen*

by U.S. Coast Guard,
Marine Board of Investigation

*As a rule, articles and books dealing with the Bermuda Tri-
angle contain brief summaries of the disappearance of ships
and planes, which, when grouped together, tend to create a
picture of mysterious forces converging and creating havoc.
Most of these narratives tend to select elements of the elusive
or even supernatural, from what are, in fact, detailed and
professional accounts of such disappearances. In order to provide our readers with a representative example of thorough
investigation, we are reprinting below the full text of a report
prepared by the U.S. Coast Guard's Marine Board of Investigation, addressed to the Coast Guard's commandant on August 23, 1963.*

*The Marine Board's report, entitled "*SS MARINE SULPHUR
QUEEN; *disappearance of at sea on or about 4 February
1963," was signed by: Rear Admiral James D. Craik, chairman of the board; Captain Benjamin D. Shoemaker, member of the board; and Commander Albert S. Frevola, member and recorder of the board. This text, from which not a
single word has been deleted, should be read in conjunction
with "Did the SS* Marine Sulphur Queen *Explode?" by Kent
Jordan, in the central section of this volume.*

1. At about 1830, CST, 2 February 1963, the SS MARINE
SULPHUR QUEEN, with a crew of 39 and a full cargo of approximately 15,260 long tons of molten sulphur, took departure from Sabine Sea Buoy on a voyage from Beaumont,
Texas to Norfolk, Virginia and subsequently disappeared at
sea without the transmission of a radio distress message.

2. The SS MARINE SULPHUR QUEEN, O.N. 245295 (EX-ESSO
NEW HAVEN) was an all-welded T2-SE-A1, tankship; of 7240
gross tons and 4057 net tons; length 504 ft., breadth 68.2 ft.,
and depth 39.2 ft.; built at Sun Shipbuilding and Drydock

Co., Chester, Pa. in 1944 and converted to a molten sulphur carrier at Bethlehem Steel Co. Shipyard, Baltimore, Md., during the latter part of 1960. The vessel was single screw, powered by a 7240 shaft horsepower turbo-electric drive manufactured by Westinghouse Elec. & Mfg. Co. The vessel was owned by Marine Sulphur Transport Corporation and operated under a bareboat charter by Marine Transport Lines, Inc., both companies being located at 11 Broadway, New York, N.Y. The conversion to a molten sulphur carrier was accomplished in accordance with plans approved by the U. S. Coast Guard and the American Bureau of Shipping.

3. The vessel was certificated by the U. S. Coast Guard at Baltimore, Md. on 18 January 1961 for the carriage of "Grade E liquids at elevated temperatures" and classed by the American Bureau of Shipping as to hull and machinery. The vessel was recertificated by the U. S. Coast Guard at Beaumont, Texas on 17 January 1963 and retained in class by the American Bureau of Shipping at the same time. The vessel had valid load line certificates, both International and Coastwise, issued by the American Bureau of Shipping and valid radio certificates issued by the Beaumont, Texas office of the Federal Communications Commission covering both the installed radio equipment and the lifeboat portable radio.

4. In general, the conversion to a molten surphur carrier consisted of the removal of all the transverse bulkheads in the way of the original T-2 centerline tanks and the installation of an independent tank 306 ft. long, 30 ft. 6 in. wide and 33 ft. high, internally divided by sulphur-tight transverse bulkheads into four tanks with No. 1 being 83 ft. long; No. 2 being 73 ft. long; No. 3 being 73 ft. long; and No. 4 being 77 ft. long. To accommodate the sulphur cargo tank it was necessary to cut away part of the original No. 1 cargo tanks, port and starboard, as well as part of the original forward bulkhead of the after pump room. The existing structure of No. 1 tanks was cut away from frame 71 forward to frame 72½ including the centerline bulkhead and the transverse bulkhead for a distance of 17 ft. 6 in. on either side of the centerline. The remaining portions of the No. 1 tanks were changed to void spaces by enclosing them with non-watertight longitudinal wing tank bulkheads. The after pump room forward bulkhead at frame 47 was cut out to permit the tank to extend into the pump room to frame 46½ and thus, in essence, the pump room became a part of the void space surrounding

144

the tank. The original wing tanks, 2 through 9 inclusive, were left intact and fitted as water ballast tanks. As the cargo tanks were loaded, the wing tanks were deballasted and the reverse procedure was followed when offloading, thus minimizing the change in draft during these operations.

5. The sulphur tank was of rectangular cross section, constructed of mild steel meeting American Bureau of Shipping requirements for steel to be welded. A longitudinal swash bulkhead ran the full length of the major tank and each of the four individual tanks were fitted with a transverse swash bulkhead at approximately their mid-length. At normal temperatures the transverse sulphur-tight bulkheads and the transverse swash bulkheads coincided with the original center tank transverse bulkheads.

6. In the construction of the tank, the sides, ends, and sulphur-tight transverse bulkheads were constructed of steel plate 7/16 in. at the top increasing to 11/16 in. plate at the bottom, all having 10 in. × 3/4 in. web frames fitted as stiffeners. The top was made of 3/8 in. plate with 8 in. × 7/16 in. web frames fitted as stiffeners. The bottom was 11/16 in. plate with 9 in. × 5/8 in. web frames fitted on the exterior thereof as stiffeners. The centerline and transverse swash bulkheads were 7/16 in. plate throughout with 8 in. × 7/16 in. web frames fitted as stiffeners. All the above stiffeners were fitted at approximate 2 ft. 6 in. frame spacing. To support the sides, ends and sulphur-tight transverse bulkheads there were installed two horizontal web plate stringers 5 ft. × 1/2 in. plate faced with a 21 in. × 1 in. plate and bracketed by a 1/2 in. plate with 3 in. flange at the 9 ft. and 18 ft. 6 in. levels. These stringers were bracketed on 7 ft. 6 in. centers, and at the normal ship frame spacing of 12 ft. 2 in., a tie beam, 12 in. × 12 in. × 1-1/4 in. web frame, was fitted from the upper stringer to the centerline swash bulkhead. At the after end of each tank there was fitted a port and starboard sump of the same thickness as the tank bottom, 2 ft. 6 in. in width and 18 in. deep near the centerline and sloping up to 5 in. near the sides. Additionally, each tank top was fitted at the after end with a port and starboard expansion trunk approximately 5 ft. square and 4 ft. in height of 1/2 in. plate which extended through the weather deck into a watertight pump house. The inboard sides of both the sumps and trunks were approximately 2 ft. 7 in. off the centerline of the ship. At the forward centerline of each tank there was fitted a 6 in. vent

leading to the weather deck and extending approximately 3 ft. above with a U-bend. The vents were steam jacketed and were fitted with stainless steel flexible piping between the tank tops and the weather deck. In each of the expansion trunks there was a 4 in. vent which terminated in a U-bend approximately 2 ft. above the top of the pump house. These vents were also steam jacketed and fitted with stainless steel flexible piping between the trunk tops and the overhead of the pump house. At the top of each expansion trunk, which was closed with 1/2 in. plate, there was fitted a 2 ft. diameter entrance scuttle and a 1 in. thick annular ring 25 in. inner diameter and 32 in. outer diameter serving as a foundation for a deep well pump electric motor.

7. In effecting the installation of the major tank, the height of the center vertical keel from frames 46½ to 72½, was cut down from 7 ft. 6 in. to a constant height of 3 ft. 4 in. and a 17 in. × 1 in. flange plate was welded to the top thereof. To accommodate the cargo tank the transverse web frames, or floors, in the bottom of the ship were cut down to a constant horizontal plane of 3 ft. 4 in. above the flat keel plate and were fitted with 15 in. × 1 in. flange plates welded to the top thereof. On either side of the centerline vertical keel the bottom longitudinals, 7 ft. 6 in. and 15 ft. off the centerline port and starboard, were extended up to this same 3 ft. 4 in. horizontal plane by the addition of 1/2 in. plate with an 8 in. × 1 in. flange plate welded to the top. The bottom of the sulphur tank was fitted with 5 longitudinal stringers of 1/2 in. plate faced with 8 in. × 1 in. flanges. The longitudinals fitted to the bottom of the tank and the flange plates of the ship's bottom longitudinals were bolted together, except between frames 58 and 60, with a 1/2 in. thick 8 in. wide phenolite laminated plastic installed between the flanges as a heat isolator. To permit free expansion and contraction of the tank, these bolts, 1 in. in diameter, were mounted in 1-1/16 in. holes in the tank longitudinals passing through 1-1/16 in. × 3-1/2 in. slots in the plastic heat isolator and the flanges in the ship's bottom longitudinals. Because of the increased expansion at either end of the tank, the slots were increased in length to 4 in. for the last 10 ft.; this increase in length of the slots was not reflected in the vessel's plans. Nuts were screwed onto the bolts hand-tight, tightened 1/4 turn and spot welded to the bolt body. All bolt holes were drilled with 10 in. centers, a single row on each of the outboard longitudinals and a double row on the centerline longitudinal. The bolts and nuts

were mild steel except for the centerline rows which were ASTM A-235, high strength material. Between frames 58 and 60, a distance of 24 ft. 4 in., the five longitudinals fitted to the bottom of the tank were welded to the five ship's bottom longitudinals after a 1/2 in. thick plate was inserted to compensate for the absence of the heat isolating material in these areas. After the conversion was completed heat was applied to the tanks, utilizing the heating coils hereinafter discussed. The air temperature within the tanks at this time was determined to be between 240° F to 252° F. While no precise measurements of the actual expansion of the tank were made at this time, one witness recalled the ends of the tank had expanded so that the bolts were within 1/4 to 3/8 of an inch from the ends of the 4" slots. During this test and later at various times during the actual operation of the vessel, loud noises were heard throughout the vessel. These noises were caused by the expansion and contraction of the tank.

8. Similarly, the centerline deck longitudinal girder was cut from its 5 ft. original depth to 2 ft. 8 in. except in the way of frames 58 to 60 where the depth was 3 ft. 6 in. and where this girder was welded directly to the top of the tank. Where the girder was cut to a depth of 2 ft. 8 in., a 15 in. × 1 in. face flange was welded to the bottom thereof. On the tank top at the centerline, there were fitted at each frame between frames 47 to 71 inclusive, except for the welded portion between frames 58 to 60, bracketed webs 1/2 in. thick with face plates 8 in. × 1 in. × 12 in. long. Here, like the bottom connection, 1 in. bolts were mounted in 1-1/16 in. holes in the tank connections up through similar slotted holes in the 1/2 in. heat isolator material and the deck girder flange plate, each connection being made with two bolts and nuts of ASTM A-235 material staggered on either side of the centerline of the deck girder.

9. At frame 59 a complete watertight bulkhead surrounded the tank so that a void space then existed fore and aft of this bulkhead. This watertight bulkhead was made up of 1/2 in. steel plate. At frames 53 and 65 diaphragm plates, 3/8 in. thick, were fitted between the tank sides and the wing tank longitudinal bulkhead, both on the port and starboard sides. These diaphragm plates extended from 4 ft. 6 in. above the tank bottom to within 1 ft. 6 in. of the top of the tank. At about the 20 ft. level above the tank bottom, access holes, port and starboard, 15 in. × 36 in. were cut out of the

diaphragm plates to permit access along a cat walk, which together with appropriate vertical ladders, permitted personnel to descend from the weather deck to the void space surrounding the tank. On each side of the tank at frames 47, 50, 56, 62, 68 and 71, tank expansion connections were fitted. These expansion connections were made up in two pieces, each 6 ft. × 1 ft. 3 in. × 1/2 in. plate faced with a 4 ft. × 12 in. × 3/4 in. flange. One piece was welded to the sulphur tank and the other to the wing tank longitudinal bulkhead. The piece welded to the sulphur tank had 8 1-1/16 in. holes and the piece welded to the wing tank had 8 2-7/16 in. horizontal slotted holes. Here again, 1/2 in. plastic heat isolator material was used between the flange plates and 1 in. mild steel bolts and nuts were fitted to join the two parts of the expansion connection. These expansion connections were located such that top of the connection was about 1 ft. 6 in. below the top of the sulphur tank.

10. To reduce thermal losses through the sulphur tank structure, the entire tank exterior was insulated with a blanket of Owens-Corning Armaglas PF-335, 4 in. thick on the bottom, sides, ends and around the expansion trunks and 6 in. thick on the top. The insulation was held in place with Nelson welding pins and covered with #18 gauge galvanized wire netting secured in place with clips over the Nelson pins. Prior to the installation of the insulation the entire tank exterior was painted with aluminum paint. The tank interior was not given any protective coating.

11. To maintain the desired temperatures within the tanks, steam heating coils made up of 2 in., schedule 80, ASTM A-53 steel pipe were fitted in the bottom, sumps, sides and ends of the tank. Tank No. 1 had 18 coils in all, 4 each in its forward end, two sides and bottom, with one coil for each of its two sumps. Tank No. 4 was similarly fitted, except the end coils were at its after end in lieu of its forward end. Tanks Nos. 2 and 3 each had 14 coils in all, since there were no end coils in these tanks. Each coil had its own individual steam supply line entering the tank at the top and leaving the tank at the bottom port side through a steam trap. The steam to these coils came from the desuperheater line from the main boilers reduced to a pressure of 35 to 40 pounds per square inch while in port; and from the 70 pounds per square inch bleed-off stage from the main turbine reduced to a pressure of 35 to 40 pounds per square inch while at sea. No

thermometers were installed in either of these two steam supply lines. The steam condensate return line to the engine room terminated in an atmospheric tank where the condensate could be sighted visually for discoloration. The heating coils were made up for a working pressure of 60 pounds per square inch and were tested hydrostatically to a pressure of 200 pounds per square inch. All shop made coil joints were electric arc welded and x-rayed; all coil joints made on the ship were gas welded. Each of the four cargo tanks were fitted with thermocouples, on the port and starboard sides, located about half way up from the tank bottom. The temperatures were automatically recorded on a tape in the engine room. Testimony was received that this recorder was inoperative during the period October 1962 to January 1963; it was then repaired and placed back in operation. The temperature recorder was not considered to be essential for the safety of the vessel because the steam pressure and the resultant temperature to the heating coils could be carefully controlled. The ship was also provided with portable recording thermometers to ascertain the temperature of the cargo.

12. As noted before, the expansion trunks in each of the four individual sulphur cargo tanks extended through the weather deck. To permit expansion an opening in the weather deck was cut out, then adequately reinforced with a doubler plate and web frame stiffeners. This cut out was of such size that a 4 in. opening was allowed all around the periphery of the trunks. This 4 in. opening was, at normal atmospheric temperatures, filled with a 4 in. layer of Armaglas insulating material which surrounded the trunks. The trunk and deck were connected by means of a canvas boot, later changed to asbestos cloth, to insure a gas tight seal and to provide the necessary flexibility when the tank moved. To insure watertight integrity of the hull, a combination pump and controller house was constructed over the expansion trunks at the after end of each cargo tank. Each house was approximately 25 ft. × 12 ft. 10 in. × 8 ft. high with a 3 ft. wide controller house on the port side incorporated therein but separated from the pump house by a watertight bulkhead. The pump room and controller room were each fitted with a watertight door. At the after end of each controller house the weather deck had a 2 ft. × 3 ft. cut out for the purpose of ventilating the voids surrounding the cargo tanks. This cut out led into a space approximately 2 ft. × 3 ft. × 6 ft. high separated from the controller room by bulkheads, and the air was discharged there-

from through a louvered opening at the rear of the house. At the original conversion each pump house had two removable plates 4 ft. × 4 ft. bolted to the top of the house to give additional ventilation at the time of loading and discharging. In June 1961 these plates were replaced with hinged watertight scuttles at Bethlehem Steel Co. Shipyard, Beaumont, Texas.

13. The vessel's cargo piping consisted of two 10 in. discharge and fill headers running athwartship of the weather deck at frame 67 that could be connected either port or starboard to Chiksan joints at the loading and discharge docks. From the headers one 10 in. line ran aft to load and discharge tanks No. 1 and No. 2; another parallel 10 in. line ran aft to load and discharge tanks No. 3 and No. 4. A 10 in. crossover line led into each of the four pump houses. From the crossover line an 8 in. fill pipe was run down through the port side expansion trunk top to within a few inches of the bottom of the tank, ending in a 90° ell. The necessary valves were installed in the system so that each tank could be filled independently. To discharge the cargo of molten sulphur each sump was fitted with a deep well pump driven by an explosion-proof electric motor, the motor being mounted on top of the expansion trunk cover. The discharge lines from the pumps were 6 in. pipe connected into the 10 in. crossover lines in the pump houses which in turn led into the 10 in. lines on deck. The discharge piping was originally fitted only with plug cocks and during one discharge operation sulphur was diverted into another cargo tank causing a spill. Following that spill, at Bethlehem Steel Co. Shipyard, Beaumont, Texas in June 1961, the discharge lines were fitted with swing check valves to prevent further spills of this nature. All cargo piping was steam jacketed by running the cargo piping through a larger pipe size; i.e. 10 in. pipe inside of 12 in. pipe, 8 in. pipe inside of 10 in. pipe, and 6 in. pipe inside of 8 in. pipe. All valves were steam jacketed as well. Stainless steel expansion joints were fitted in the loading and discharge piping within the cargo pump houses, these being steam coil wrapped. All cargo piping was schedule 40, ASTM A-53 steel pipe.

14. Upon the completion of the installation of the main sulphur tank and its insulation, there existed a void space fore and aft of frame 59 completely surrounding the tank. At the sides approximately 2 ft. of space existed, at the bottom approximately 3 ft. 6 in. of space existed, at the top approx-

imately 3 ft. of space existed, and at the ends approximately 6 ft. of space existed. The bottom vertical foundation girders and the main deck girder all had lightening holes which permitted the free movement of air across the bottom and top of the tank. Power ventilation was installed utilizing two 11,000 cubic feet per minute fans in each of the two void spaces. These fans with explosion-proof and watertight electric motors, were mounted on the starboard side of the weather deck at frames 53, 59, 60 and 65, and discharged air through ventilation ducts near the bottom of the cargo tank; the air then swept under the tank and was discharged as previously described in paragraph 12, through the openings cut out of the weather deck in the controller houses. The original king post ventilators located, port and starboard, at frame 47 and extending down into the after pump room, now a part of the void, were left intact, except that all sheet metal ducting below the weather deck was removed. The dampers in these king posts were kept in the "closed" position at all times and just prior to the last voyage the cowls were removed and canvas covers were installed.

15. Relative to the fixed fire extinguishing system fitted on the MARINE SULPHUR QUEEN the original fire main was left intact as built, and the steam smothering system was modified as necessary to provide protection to the sulphur cargo tanks. At the time of conversion, the original steam smothering system to all cargo tanks was removed and a new installation was made to the four sulphur cargo tanks. Essentially, the new cargo tank system consisted of a run of 2 in. pipe from the main steam smothering line to a header at each tank at frames 67½, 64½, 56, and 50 respectively from which four 1½ in. branch lines penetrated the weather deck and then led into the top of the four cargo tanks. In addition, steam smothering was piped to the void space on either side of the cargo tanks at frames 64½ and 52½. During the first year of operation it was found that the sulphur was plugging up the nozzles where they entered the sulphur tank top, so at the shipyard availability in February 1962, the system was altered. This alteration consisted of leading new piping to the cargo tanks at each of the expansion trunks. The piping was led from the deck line, through each of the four pump houses and thence into the top of the trunks. Additionally, a clean out fitting was installed in each piping lead. The old piping penetrating at the weather deck into the cargo tanks was disconnected and blanked off at the weather deck. The new sys-

tem was tested to the satisfaction of a U. S. Coast Guard inspector.

16. At the time of the conversion certain renewals and repairs of the vessel's structural parts were accomplished. Keel plates Nos. 5, 6, 7 and 14 were renewed, all deck longitudinals in way of the sulphur cargo tank were renewed, and all deck longitudinals and transverse web frames in the wing tanks were renewed as necessary. Flat bar stiffeners in way of No. 3 wing tank vertical brackets, port and starboard, were installed to strengthen these structural members. Additional repairs consisted of building up erroded welding in bottom plates, repair of a fracture in the stern frame skeg, and repair of scattered leaking welds in the rudder plates.

17. In October 1961, the MARINE SULPHUR QUEEN was at the Bethlehem Steel Company yard, Beaumont, Texas for repair of storm damage allegedly sustained during hurricane "Carla" on 7, 8 and 9 September 1961, while enroute from Beaumont, Texas to Carteret, New Jersey. This damage consisted essentially of fractures in web frames, bilge brackets, shell longitudinals and bulkheads in the way of No. 5 wing tanks, port and starboard; No. 7 wing tanks, port and starboard; No. 9 wing tanks, port and starboard; and No. 3 port, No. 2 starboard, and No. 4 port wing tanks. At this time an 18 in. fracture was found in shell plate "F" strake at web frame No. 61. All fractures were repaired as necessary. Testimony was received that this fractured shell plate was replaced in February 1962.

18. In February 1962 the vessel underwent U. S. Coast Guard reinspection and was also drydocked at that time at the Bethlehem Steel Co. yard at Beaumont, Texas. During this period the bulbous bow section was repaired and internals cropped out and replaced as necessary. All sea chests and sea valves were opened up for examination and the necessary repairs or renewals were made; including the renewal of two 4 in. sanitary valves in the shaft alley and the 24 in. main condenser discharge valve. The tailshaft was drawn, subjected to a magnetic particle examination and found satisfactory; the liner was lightly scored and a light polish cut was taken on the liner; stern tube bearing was renewed, and the stern tube gland was repacked. Upon completion of this yard availability the vessel was found to be seaworthy by both the U. S. Coast Guard and the American Bureau of Shipping.

19. On 16 January 1963 the vessel, while loading cargo at Beaumont, Texas, commenced U. S. Coast Guard biennial inspection for certification. The general alarm system, steering gear, engine telegraph, fire hose, navigation light panel were tested and found satisfactory; all portable fire extinguishers were serviced and found satisfactory; life preservers were examined and found satisfactory; 11 of 18 ring buoys were replaced; lifeboats were examined and repairs thereto completed to satisfaction of the inspector; all accessible spaces were examined and found satisfactory; port boiler opened up and fire side and water side and boiler mounting examined and found satisfactory; hydrostatic test held on port boiler and found all tight; all machinery examined and tested as necessary to prove satisfactory. The vessel was issued a new Certificate of Inspection to expire on 17 January 1965 and a Form CG-835 "Notice of Requirements" issued to the Master. On 1-2 February 1963 the vessel was again boarded in Beaumont and the starboard boiler and mountings were examined and found satisfactory; boiler was hydrostatically tested and found tight. The remaining outstanding requirements against the ship at this time, to be completed at next drydocking or within 90 days, whichever is sooner, were:

"(a) Replace or repair relief valve on ship's service air compressor.

(b) Make permanent repairs to various lube oil cooling and motor cooling lines, main condenser by-pass and other lines as outlined by C. G. Inspector."

At the same time as the above U. S. Coast Guard inspection, the American Bureau of Shipping made the regular annual survey on hull, machinery and boilers, and upon completion thereof the vessel was found to be seaworthy and fit to retain her present class with the American Bureau of Shipping. The load line certificate was endorsed by the American Bureau of Shipping Surveyor on 1 February 1963. The Officer in Charge, Federal Comunications Commission, Beaumont, Texas, inspected the radio equipment installed on the vessel, together with the lifeboat portable radio on 3 January 1963 and found all satisfactory.

20. During the operation of the vessel between 18 January 1961 and its disappearance in February 1963, testimony from previous crew members disclosed that there had been

numerous fires on board the MARINE SULPHUR QUEEN. A review of the ship's deck and engine room smooth logs disclosed mention of four specific fires and the use of the steam smothering system on 8 other days, which substantiates this testimony. These log entries were made on 24 August 1961, 7 October 1961, 8 October 1961, 15 February 1962, 16 October 1962, 20 October 1962, 3 November 1962, 22 December 1962, 26 December 1962, 27 December 1962, 28 December 1962 and 29 December 1962. All of these reported fires occurred in the void space with the exception of the fire logged on 24 August 1961. This latter entry concerned a possible fire within No. 3 cargo tank while the vessel was discharging at Carteret, New Jersey. However a later examination of the tank disclosed no evidence that there had been a fire therein. The fires in the void spaces were described as having occurred in the tank insulation, of "pie" shape and size. These fires were usually not completely extinguished by the use of the steam smothering system. In almost all cases either the Master or a crew member, using a fresh air mask, descended into the void space and finally extinguished these fires by dousing them with fresh water. The source of ignition of these fires was not determined. These previous crew members testified that there was little or no apprehension on their part of any danger as a result of these fires. In addition they testified that the general alarm was not sounded at any time.

21. The vessel suffered one incident of grounding. This occurred at Tampa, Florida on 13 October 1961 when she grounded twice; the first time she was aground from 0523 to 0804, the second time she was aground from 0915 to 1440. The American Bureau of Shipping issued a "Certificate of Seaworthiness" on 13 October 1961 following this incident. On 29 January 1962 the vessel was in drydock at Beaumont, Texas and the damage alleged to have occurred in this grounding consisted of:

(a) 3 of the 4 blades of the propeller nicked in various amounts
(b) Fairwater missing
(c) Rudder side plating fractured in several locations
(d) Tailshaft subject to shock

All of the above were satisfactorily repaired at that drydocking, except that in the case of the tailshaft no damage was found.

22. There were three minor collisions reported in the ship's logs, none of which resulted in any significant damage.

23. Two instances of storm damage and two significant instances of operation in heavy weather were found in the vessel's logs:

(a) On 28 January 1961 heavy weather was encountered which damaged the insulation on the cargo piping located on the main deck when seas swept over the bow. The insulation was originally protected by a covering of canvas. As a result of this damage, at the Bethlehem Steel Co. shipyard, Beaumont, Texas in June 1961, all the cargo piping on the main deck was covered with thin aluminum sheets and a breakwater was installed just forward of the cargo manifold for further protection.

(b) The vessel was at sea during hurricane "Carla" on 7, 8, and 9 September 1961 and the damage sustained at that time has been discussed in paragraph 17 above.

This particular voyage commenced at Beaumont, Texas on 5 September 1961. Log entries for the three days of "Carla" showed winds of up to force 9, Beaufort Scale, and the seas were described as "very rough." At 1245, 7 September 1961, the log shows that the vessel was turned about to the reciprocal course, but no entry was found as to when the vessel again resumed its original course.

(c) The vessel suffered no other storm damage, but one entry of particular interest was found in the log of 4 March 1962, which states, "From 1747, 3-2-62 to 0630, 3-4-62, vessel on various reduced speeds to ease vessel in high seas and very deep swells noted to put racking stress on the vessel. A thorough search of compartments to be made to ascertain if vessel suffered damage as a result of this heavy weather." The log indicates that during this period the vessel encountered force 7 winds with very rough seas primarily from nearly dead ahead. The log fails to reveal that the vessel sustained any damage as a result of the heavy weather.

(d) The vessel also encountered hurricane "Ella," 18, 19
and 20 October 1962 along the Atlantic coast line
with winds and seas primarily from dead ahead, maximum force 7, seas very rough. No damage was reported as having been found.

24. There was one incident of machinery failure which occurred on 9 February 1962 when on the first day out from
Beaumont, Texas, the outboard auxiliary generator failed.
The vessel returned to Beaumont and a reconditioned unit
was installed on 14 February 1962. The inboard auxiliary
generator was tested that same day and megger readings
were found to be low. As a result, this generator was replaced by a reconditioned unit on 27 February 1962 at Beaumont, Texas.

25. The cargo tank insulation was contaminated with sulphur
on the following occasions:

(a) A major sulphur spill occurred on 8 April 1961 when,
during discharge of cargo at Carteret, New Jersey,
the cargo pumps in No. 1 tank tripped out and the
cargo pumps from No. 2 tank pushed sulphur into the
No. 1 tank, causing it to overflow. To rid the No. 1
pump house of the spilled sulphur, the crew punched
holes in the canvas boots around the expansion trunks
and the sulphur flowed down and onto the tank insulation. Approximately 4500 sq. ft. of insulation
found to be impregnated by the overflow was replaced
at the shipyard on or about 6 June 1961. At the same
time, solidified sulphur, 10 in. deep covering 100 sq.
ft. on the ship's bottom in the vicinity of No. 1 tank;
and 8 in. deep covering 400 sq. ft. between frames 63
and 66 in the way of No. 2 tank was removed.

(b) On 28 December 1961, while discharging sulphur the
cargo pipe expansion joint in No. 3 pump house
leaked and the crew rid the pump house of sulphur by
punching holes in the canvas boots around the expansion trunks with resultant sulphur penetration of the
tank insulation. This insulation was replaced at the
shipyard in February 1962.

26. In the latter part of 1961 a crack was found in the after
end of No. 4 cargo tank, starboard side in the way of the

weld of the sump to the tank bottom. This crack also permitted sulphur to impregnate the tank insulation. This leak was of such size that sulphur accumulated in the ship's bottom in that area to a depth of several inches. The ship's crew was engaged in its removal on several voyages prior to its repair at Beaumont during the shipyard availability in February 1962. During this availability, the crack described as about 12 in. in length and of an undetermined width was veed out, welded on both sides and a 1/2 in. × 4 in. × 14 in. doubler was welded on the inside of the tank. The insulation replaced at this time totaled approximately 4,000 sq. ft. Another crack later developed in the same general area as that described above, and this time was to be repaired at the vessel's next availability period, on or about March 1963. The sulphur from this leak accumulated in the ship's bottom and was variously estimated to be in the amount of 20 to 70 tons. This crack was peened over by the Chief Engineer in Beaumont while loading cargo for the voyage commencing on 2 February 1963 and found tight. Testimony was received from several of the previous crew members of the MARINE SULPHUR QUEEN that on numerous occasions, while on loaded voyages in a heavy seaway, sulphur would spew out of the forward 6-inch cargo tank vents. The molten sulphur, on striking the weather deck, would freeze and accumulate to a depth of a foot or more under the vents. Also, in some instances, the sulphur would build up inside the vents, even though fitted with steam heated coils. Following such a spill it was necessary to chip the sulphur off the deck and to strike the vents with a hammer to free them of the sulphur.

27. An inclining test of the MARINE SULPHUR QUEEN was performed on 14 January 1961 under U. S. Coast Guard supervision. On 19 January 1961 the vessel was issued a temporary stability letter by the Officer in Charge, Marine Inspection, Baltimore, Maryland that stated in part that: "The 'Preliminary Trim, Stability and Load Stress Booklet' for T-2 Sulphur Tanker SS MARINE SULPHUR QUEEN prepared by Bethlehem Steel Shipbuilding Division, Baltimore, Maryland, dated January 1961 and bearing U. S. Coast Guard approval stamp dated 19 January 1961 is applicable on a temporary basis to subject vessel. The hull stress information contained in the booklet has been furnished voluntarily by the company and while not requiring Coast Guard approval should be strictly adhered to by the Master. Operation of the vessel under loading conditions which result in a hogging (or sagging)

numeral in excess of the 100 level is not authorized." A naval architect, an employee of the operators of the vessel, was requested by the Board to make loading stress calculations for all voyages. Due to the lack of specific cargo loading figures for the first four voyages, calculations for these voyages could not be made. However, of the remaining 60 voyages, it was calculated that while in a loaded condition the sagging numeral exceeded 100 in 52 instances varying from 100.55 to 104.66. The hogging numeral on all fully loaded voyages varied from 47.63 to 55.01 with increased numerals of up to 91.27 when in a partially loaded condition. While in ballast the numerals did not exceed 100 at any time. The calculated stress numerals at the time of the vessel's departure from Beaumont, Texas on 2 February 1963 were 54.37 in hog and 101.01 in sag. On the other hand, the company naval architect and the Coast Guard naval architect both testified that in their opinion this repeated small over-stress in sag was not significant. However, they both agreed that it would have been preferable to operate the vessel at or below the 100 stress numeral at all times.

28. During the period from September through December 1961, the Master was ordered by the operating company to experiment with ballasting arrangements in order to reduce the departure draft from the discharge port. Prior to this period, wing tanks 2 through 8, port and starboard, were pressed up. In this three month period, the ballast arrangement was 2, 4, 5, 6 and 8 wing tanks, port and starboard, pressed up and the remainder empty. The hog and sag stress numeral was computed for these voyages, 7 in number; the hog stress numeral varied between 71.91 and 74.48, and the sag stress numeral varied between 72.88 and 75.00. On one voyage only, wing tanks 2, 4, 6 and 8, port and starboard, were pressed up and on that voyage the hog stress numeral was 88.74 and the sag stress numeral was 57.85. At the conclusion of this three month experimental period the vessel was ballasted as before filling all wing tanks. In any event, it was found necessary to fill all wing tanks prior to arrival at Beaumont, Texas so that the vessel's draft would permit making up the cargo loading joints.

29. Considerable testimony was received from the operating company personnel pertaining to instructions to the Master, requirements and reports of shipboard safety meetings, and

the duties and responsibilities of company personnel with respect to the vessel. This testimony brought out that the MARINE SULPHUR QUEEN was treated as a normal T-2 type tankship even though the cargo, molten sulphur, in such an unusual vessel arrangement and quantity was a "first" for Marine Transport Lines. No one in the company office was assigned specifically to become knowledgeable with respect to the properties and carriage of molten sulphur. This aspect was left to the judgment of the senior officers aboard the vessel, namely the Master, Chief Mate and Chief Engineer, all of whom spent several days at the Beaumont plant of Texas Gulf Sulphur Co. The Master was not provided any specific instructions with respect to molten sulphur and in fact, he received only the same letter of designation as Master and the same general instructions issued by the company to masters of all its tank vessels. With relation to the "Trim, Stability and Loading Booklet" prepared by the Bethlehem Steel Co. shipyard, Baltimore, dated January 1961, the Master received no guidance as to its use and no requirement was placed upon him to report to the company the loading numerals for each voyage. Further no one in the company ever made any independent calculations of such numerals. However, it was determined that there was a requirement for such reports by masters of tankers which the company operated under an operating contract with the Military Sea Transportation Service. The company officials were also questioned extensively on the subject of the fires that had been testified to by previous crew members. A few of these fires were known to these officials but apparently they never required a full report with respect thereto from the master, nor did they otherwise make any attempt to determine the possible cause of these fires. However, the vessel was visited at irregular intervals by port engineers and port captains employed by the company who on these occasions did conduct inspections of various parts of the vessel. Further, the company had an active safety program with membership comprised of personnel from the Operations Department, Marine Department, Personnel Department and the Personal Injuries Section. Shipboard safety meeting minutes were received in the Operations Department and copies made for each committee member. Files of the MARINE SULPHUR QUEEN contained only the minutes of three such shipboard meetings. These minutes, except for the mention of one fire, were found to have no bearing on this casualty.

30. The Board received testimony from three chemists on the properties of molten sulphur. While there were minor conflicts in their testimony, it was determined that molten sulphur is a relatively safe product to store and handle. Further, molten sulphur has been transported for more than two decades in railway tank cars, pipe lines, tank trucks, and barges. Transportation by ship is a relatively new operation, having had its inception approximately five years ago when a Liberty type vessel had independent tanks installed in two of its cargo holds. Pipe lines and storage tanks constructed of mild steel, used for many years to contain molten sulphur, have been found on inspection to evidence no appreciable amounts of corrosion.

31. Numerous studies have been made on the property of molten sulphur, and the results thereof have been published in various trade periodicals and manuals. There is general agreement that molten sulphur has a freezing point of approximately 238° F, and since its viscosity increases abruptly above a temperature of about 318° F it is normally handled at temperatures between 250° and 310° F. The density of molten sulphur at 250° F is approximately 112.6 pounds per cubic foot which decreases slightly with an increase in temperature and/or the presence of hydrocarbon impurities.

32. These studies show that all naturally occurring sulphur contains small quantities of hydrocarbon impurities. These react with the sulphur to produce hydrogen sulphide and carbon disulphide. In a quiescent state, such as in a storage tank, these two gases are liberated at a very slow rate and moderate venting ordinarily prevents the buildup of an explosive mixture even though both gases are heavier than air. Agitation or aeration of molten sulphur, however, can result in a rapid liberation of the two gases; under such conditions a poisonous and explosive atmosphere can be formed.

33. The Bureau of Mines pamphlet 6185 entitled "Gas Explosion Hazards Associated with the Bulk Storage of Molten Sulphur" describes tests to determine (1) the nature and rate of release of such vapors by commercial molten sulphur, and (2) the flammability characteristics of these vapors. Experiments were conducted with both bright and dark sulphurs in a laboratory closed system and in two commercial storage tanks. Neither grade of sulphur was identified as to its carbon content. In the laboratory closed system a one pound sample of dark sulphur produced the following results:

Time in Hours	Cumulative Volume in Milliliters	
	Hydrogen Sulphide	Carbon Disulphide
20	0.009	0.052
105	4.10	0.186
175	9.05	0.332
239	12.51	0.425

Bright sulphur produced the following results:

Time in Hours	Cumulative Volume in Milliliters	
	Hydrogen Sulphide	Carbon Disulphide
23	0.002	None
48	0.002	None
118	0.004	None
280	0.005	None

From an analysis of the vapor space in the two commercial storage tanks in which the sulphur had been stored for 14 days, the dark sulphur showed 0.29 volume-percent of hydrogen sulphide and 0.02 volume-percent of carbon disulphide. For bright sulphur these readings were 0.12 for hydrogen sulphide and a trace of carbon disulphide. The low concentrations of the gases found in these storage tanks, as compared with the concentrations obtained in the laboratory closed system, are attributed to the use of vented tanks even though both gases are heavier than air. In unvented tanks with small vapor spaces, the concentration of these gases would be higher. Further, although the gases were fairly well mixed in these storage tanks it is considered possible that layering could occur under certain conditions. In this eventuality flammable mixtures would then be formed more quickly than if these gases were thoroughly mixed. With a 2.8 volume-percent of carbon disulphide the spontaneous ignition (auto-ignition) temperatures were determined for carbon disulphide in hydrogren sulphide air atmospheres. It was found that with 0% hydrogen sulphide the carbon disulphide ignites at 212° F and this auto-ignition temperature gradually increases to 356° F with 2.5 volume-percent of hydrogen sulphide. Thus, an increase in the hydrogen sulphide content increases the auto-ignition temperature of the mixture. At the same time an increase in ambient temperature requires an increase in the hydrogen sulphide concentration to suppress ignition. Auto-ignition will occur only if the combustible concentration exceeds the lower limit of flammability (about 1 percent). The minimum concentration of carbon disulphide in air necessary to auto-ignite at 275° F was found to be 1.4 volume-percent; with this concentration of carbon disulphide, 0.05 volume-percent of hydrogen sulphide was sufficient to suppress ignition. The laboratory results with the dark sulphur indicate that initially, carbon disulphide was evolved at a higher rate than was hydrogen sulphide. After approximately one day in the molten state, however, the evolution rate of carbon disulphide decreased and that of hydrogen sulphide continued for several days. The end result was that at first the vapors were rich in carbon disulphide, but later they were rich in hydrogen sulphide. This situation would create two different types of explosion hazards. The first explosion hazard could exist if sufficient carbon disulphide vapors are present in a storage tank; the vapors could then ignite spontaneously, for the auto-ignition temperature of this combustible is only 212° F and the steam coils in tanks are maintained in the range of 275° - 300° F. However, the spontaneous ignition of carbon disulphide would probably only occur shortly after filling a tank with fresh molten sulphur, for the spontaneous ignition of the carbon disulphide would be suppressed by the hydrogen sulphide which is also formed at these elevated temperatures. The second explosion hazard could exist during long-term storage in a closed system. Specifically, this hazard could be created as the hydrogen sulphide builds up to its lower concentration limit of flammability; as the vapor space is decreased, the time required to reach the lower limit concentration is also decreased. In the case of hydrogen sulphide in a tank with an air-to-sulphur height ratio of 0.1, the lower limit would be reached after the second day of storage; if the height ratio is increased to 0.7, six days would be required to reach the lower limit. In conclusion, this Bureau of Mines report states that sulphur in itself does not create an explosion hazard under the conditions found in the commercial handling of molten sulphur. However, a flame initiated by the ignition of carbon disulphide or a flame propagating through a flammable hydrogen sulphide and air mixture could in turn ignite the molten sulphur. With respect to these gases evolved from molten sulphur, the experts agreed that there is no completely accurate device perfected to date that will measure the explosivity of atmospheres over liquid sulphur.

34. The Board received in evidence, a paper entitled "Safe Handling of Molten Sulphur" presented by J. R. Donovan, Monsanto Chemical Co., to the St. Louis Section of the American Institute of Chemical Engineers. In this paper, Mr. Donovan discussed three case histories of fires and moderate energy explosions involving molten sulphur.

(a) In the first case a barge was being loaded with molten sulphur. The filling nozzle for the barge tank did not extend into the tank. An explosion occurred in one of its tanks. At the time of the explosion the vapor space in the tank was approximately 4 feet. The hatch cover was not fastened and blew off, the deck over the tank was bulged upward about one foot and the tank wall was split. Approximately 65 tons of sulphur were blown through this split into the barge interior. There were no personal casualties and material damage was estimated at $50,000.00. The cause of the explosion was not definitely determined. It was surmised that the free falling sulphur released hydrogen sulphide rapidly enough to build up an explosive mixture with air in the ullage space. The source of ignition of this explosive atmosphere was surmised to be an electrostatic spark generated by the falling stream of sulphur; possible use of superheated steam in the heating coils within the tank; or by pyrophoric iron sulphide present on the tank walls.

(b) In the second case, molten sulphur was being transferred from a barge to a tank truck. Shortly after transfer began there was a minor flash and burning sulphur was ejected from the open dome of the tank truck. Some of this burning sulphur hit the terminal attendant and the truck driver who were standing on a platform about ten feet from the truck. There was no material damage to the truck. The surface of the sulphur in the tank truck was burning and was immediately put out using a steam hose. As in the first case, free falling sulphur was believed to have liberated hydrogen sulphide and the flow of sulphur built up an electrostatic charge to trigger the explosion.

(c) In this third case, a 2000 ton storage tank was being filled from a tank truck when an explosion occurred within the tank. The conical cover of the tank, 40 feet in diameter, was blown 57 feet above the top of the tank and did considerable damage in falling. There were no personal injuries. On the day of the explosion the tank contained about 1600 tons of molten sulphur. The four inch top vent had been checked that day and was clear. No cause for this explosion was given.

35. The Board also received information concerning an explosion on a foreign flag T-2 type tank vessel which had been converted to a molten sulphur carrier similar to the MARINE SULPHUR QUEEN. However, due to channel depths, this vessel could only load a partial cargo resulting in a vapor space within the tanks of about two feet in Nos. 1, 3 and 4 tanks and 12 feet in No. 2 tank. The Master's statement with respect to this explosion was: "June 27, 1962—at 0432 an explosive-like report was heard and a violent shock was felt throughout the vessel, lasting about five seconds. At that time also heavy sulphur fumes were seen coming from No. 3 cargo tank forward vent, which same comes up through No. 2 pump room. This pump room, when opened, was filled with sulphur fumes. In about 15 minutes the emission of fumes from No. 3 tank vent became normal. Some sulphur fumes were observed coming from No. 2 cofferdam (void) forward manhole, but were quickly dissipated on opening the after manhole cover, so creating a draft. No. 2 cofferdam (void) was then inspected, and it was found that No. 3 cargo tank sides from frames 57 to 58½ upper part were bulging outwards to extent of about 10 in. on both sides. Opening and inspecting from other manholes, it was noted that the top of No. 3 tank over the bulging parts appeared to be slightly indented. All pumps were run and found working. Heating coils showed no leakage. Vent lines were all clear, cargo temperatures normal, and cofferdams (voids), fore and aft, completely dry." No personal casualties resulted from this explosion and material damage was approximately $160,000. The material damage suffered was confined almost solely to the sides, top, and bottom of No. 3 cargo tank. The sides, top and bottom of the tank were bulged out; the side, top and bottom tank stiffeners were buckled; and, the swash bulkheads and stiffeners were buckled. Of particular interest to this Board was the description of the venting on the cargo tanks of this foreign vessel, which was modified following this explosion. Each tank is fitted at its forward and after end on the centerline, with an 8 in. pipe steam-jacketed vent, terminating in an inverted "U" shape approximately 24 inches above the level of the top of the pump houses. The vent at the after end of No. 2 tank and the vent at the forward end of No. 3 tank are both made up to a 10 in. pipe vent which

is unlagged but which is heated internally with a steam line; this vent extends approximately 30 ft. above the deck. Its purpose is to create a "chimney effect," inviting a flow of air over the surface of the molten sulphur in No. 2 and 3 cargo tanks. It has been reported that the vent has achieved the desired effect, and observed to be very definitely conducting great quantities of fumes from the two tanks so fitted. There have been no further reported explosions on this vessel.

36. The MARINE SULPHUR QUEEN commenced loading a full cargo of molten sulphur at 1915, 1 February 1963 and completed loading at 0600, 2 February 1963. The cargo loaded was as follows:

Tank No.	Temp. °F	Tons	Ullage	Type	Carbon Content
1	273	4135	2.31 ft.	Dark	0.14
2	274	3640	2.09 ft.	Dark	0.14
3	274	3637	2.16 ft.	Bright	0.04
4	276	3848	2.15 ft.	Bright	0.04
		15,260			

As the vessel was completing the U.S. Coast Guard inspection of the starboard boiler and the port engineer was attending to several minor crew complaints, the vessel did not depart Beaumont, Texas until 1330, 2 February 1963. In addition to the full cargo, the vessel had on board 3830 barrels of fuel, 100 tons of water and the draft in fresh water was 29 ft. 11 in. forward and 32 ft. 9 in. aft. The vessel proceeded to sea under the direction of a licensed pilot. During the approximate 4½ hours he was aboard, the pilot stated that there was no difficulty with the steering gear, gyro compass or engines. The pilot departed the vessel at the Sabine Bar Sea Buoy sometime between 1800 and 1830 CST, 2 February 1963. The departure message from the MARINE SULPHUR QUEEN to the operating company, Marine Transport Lines, advised that the vessel departed the sea buoy at 1900 CST, route Sabine, Texas direct via 24.4°N 83.0°W to 24.8°N 80.2°W to 31.2°N 79.2°W to 35.1°N 75.3°W to Cape Henry, Virginia with an estimated time of arrival at Norfolk at 1200 noon, EST, 7 February. The master of the vessel had been instructed to give both a 48 hour and 24 hour advance notice of arrival to the Norfolk agent.

37. The vessel at the time of her departure on the instant voyage was properly manned by personnel holding the requisite U. S. Coast Guard licenses and documents. In addition, the Master, licensed officers, and key unlicensed crew members, with minor exceptions, had all experienced previous service aboard the vessel and appeared to be reasonably qualified to competently discharge their duties. There is no evidence to indicate that any crew member was lacking in loyalty to the vessel.

38. At 0125 EST, 4 February 1963 a personal message from a crew member was transmitted by the vessel and received by RCA Radio. At this time the estimated position of the ship was 25°45′N, 86°W, based on an estimated speed of advance of 14.5 knots. Commencing at 1123, 4 February, RCA Radio commenced the first of two unsuccessful attempts to contact the vessel by radio. At this time the MARINE SULPHUR QUEEN if she had continued on her voyage would have been at an estimated position of 24°40′N, 83°19′W. The weather the vessel probably encountered is indicated by two exhibits received in evidence. At noon on 3 February, the SS TEXACO CALIFORNIA was at position 26°57.5′N, 88°20′W in the Gulf of Mexico on a voyage to Port Arthur, Texas where it arrived on the following day. At this same time the estimated position of the MARINE SULPHUR QUEEN was 27°12′N, 89°W, approximately 40 miles distant. The log of the TEXACO CALIFORNIA indicates that on 3 February the vessel experienced generally northerly winds from force 6 to 11, Beaufort Scale, very rough northerly seas and her decks were awash. The hindcast prepared by the U. S. Navy Oceanographic Office on the weather conditions prevailing along the projected track of the MARINE SULPHUR QUEEN during the period, 2000 EST, 3 February to 1300 EST, 4 February for the area between 88°W to 82°W indicates that the vessel may have encountered seas with a maximum wave height of 16.5 feet slightly abaft the port beam. Additionally, the winds would have been generally northerly in direction with a maximum force of 25 knots and gusting to 46 knots, also slightly abaft the vessel's port beam. The vessel's period of roll has been calculated to be of 8.5 seconds. The period of the waves was included in the hindcast and was within 10% of the vessel's period of roll.

39. The first information that the MARINE SULPHUR QUEEN was overdue was received by the Commander, Fifth Coast

Guard District at 2100 EST, 7 February 1963. This information was immediately sent to the Rescue Coordination Center, U. S. Coast Guard Commander Eastern Area in New York via "hot line." At 2145 EST the Eastern Area Rescue Coordination Center was called by a representative of the Marine Transport Lines, New York Office, reporting that the vessel was overdue, together with a description of the vessel. At 2218 EST, 7 February, the Commander Eastern Area initiated a communication check by an "All Ships Urgent Broadcast" which was repeated three times daily until 16 February 1963. At 2220 EST, 7 February, RCA Radio was contacted as to information on delivery of message to and from the vessel during the period 2-7 February, with the results previously stated.

40. Based on the above, a surface and air search was planned to commence at 0800 EST, 8 February providing that the communication check failed to locate the vessel. At 0138 EST, Coast Guard units in the 5th, 7th, and 8th Coast Guard Districts were alerted as to the search plan, and at 0800 EST when the communication check was negative, the search was commenced. The search comprised the following:

8 February—Day search—trackline from Beaumont through Florida Straits to Norfolk, a distance of 1630 miles. Seven aircraft were used in 72 flight hours, searching about 58,000 square miles. This trackline search covered 30 miles on either side of the vessel's estimated track.

8-9 February—Night search—three aircraft flew 23 flight hours and searched 22,000 square miles.

9 February—Day search—since vessel was not found along proposed track, a considerably expanded search plan was used. Nineteen aircraft flew 114 flight hours and searched 95,000 square miles.

9-10 February—Night search—two aircraft flew 12 flight hours and searched 8,300 square miles.

10 February—Day search—nineteen aircraft flew 136 flight hours and searched 76,700 square miles.

11 February—Day search—fourteen aircraft flew 86 flight hours and searched 55,000 square miles.

12 February—Day search—ten aircraft flew 42 flight
hours and searched 22,000 square miles.

13 February—Day search—two aircraft flew 16 flight
hours and searched 11,000 square miles.

This concluded the initial search for the MARINE SULPHUR
QUEEN. During the period 8-13 February 1963, Coast
Guard, Navy, Marine Corps and Air Force aircraft participated in 83 sorties, flying 499.6 hours and searched a total of
348,400 square miles with negative results. Further efforts to
locate the MARINE SULPHUR QUEEN during this initial search
utilized the Coast Guard Atlantic Merchant Vessel Reporting
system which located 42 vessels that could possibly have
sighted the MARINE SULPHUR QUEEN on 4 and 5 February.
All of these vessels were checked out by Coast Guard personnel with negative results. Several telephone calls were received by Coast Guard units during this initial search phase
with information that the ship would be found in Cuba or in
Puerto Rico. These leads were checked out by other Federal
agencies with negative results.

41. On 20 February, a U. S. Navy torpedo retriever boat operating about 12 miles southwest of Key West, Florida
sighted and picked up a fog horn and life jacket stencilled
with the vessel's name. The second phase of the search for
the MARINE SULPHUR QUEEN was then instituted, confined primarily to the area just west of Dry Tortugas Island, thence
through the Straits of Florida, along the axis of the Gulf
Stream, including the Bahamas Islands, and the east coast of
Florida to Cape Canaveral. This search with seven ships and
48 aircraft sorties flying 271.4 hours covered an additional
59,868 square miles. The probability of sighting during both
search phases was computed to be 95% for a vessel, 70% for
a metal lifeboat and 65% for a liferaft. The U.S. Navy conducted an underwater search for the vessel's hulk during the
period of 20 February through 13 March in an area from the
shoals to the 100 fathom curve between Key West and
24°35'N, 83°30'W, using six Navy vessels for 523 hours on
the scene and 17 aircraft sorties flying 57 hours with possibility of detection of 80% for the hulk. During this period, additional debris was recovered and identified as coming from the
MARINE SULPHUR QUEEN. At 1740 EST, 14 March 1963,
having received negative reports from all participating units,
the search for the vessel was discontinued.

42. The material recovered and identified as from the MARINE SULPHUR QUEEN consisted of 8 life jackets, 5 life rings, 2 name boards, 1 shirt, 1 piece of an oar, 1 storm oil can, 1 gasoline can, 1 cone buoy, and 1 fog horn. This material was deposited with the Coast Guard at Miami, Florida and later shipped to Washington, D. C. where it was examined by experts from the Bureau of Standards, the Coast Guard, and the Bureau of Fisheries. The consensus of opinion was that possibly two life jackets had been worn by persons and that the shirt tied to a life jacket had also been worn by a person. Numerous tears on the life jackets indicated attack by predatory fish. Further examination was made of certain of the debris by the Federal Bureau of Investigation who determined that the shirt bore no laundry marks, visible or invisible, and that no trace of sulphur particles was evident on any of the material. Visual examination of the material disclosed no trace of either explosion or fire.

43. On 29 April 1963, the Coast Guard Air Detachment, Corpus Christi was given a note that was reported to have been in a whiskey bottle found on or before that date by a Spanish-speaking man in Laguna Madre, near Corpus Christi at approximate position 27°39.5′N, 97°15.4′W. The bottle was broken to get the note out. A search for pieces of the bottle at that time were negative. However, the Board received the bottom of the purported bottle with no sealife attached thereto on 13 June 1963. This note written with ball point pen on a piece of manila paper, similar to a paper bag, was unsigned and referred to an explosion and two men hurt. The piece of paper also had a crude map of the Gulf of Mexico, Florida Straits and Cuba with a circle surrounding an "X", and the word "SHIP." This "X" was near the western approach to the Florida Straits. The note was turned over to a Federal examiner of questioned documents who stated in his opinion, based upon crew signatures and a letter from one crew member to his sister, that it was written by a particular crew member. The matter of this note in the bottle was also referred to the Coast and Geodetic Survey, Washington, D.C., and the Director of that agency stated that the bottle could not possibly have reached the Corpus Christi area if the bottle was dropped into the water at any place east of 85°W, unless a strong southeasterly wind had been blowing for several days before and after the dropping.

44. The following is a complete crew list of the vessel:

Name	Position	Z Number	Next of Kin	Address
1. James V. Fanning	Master	94295	Wf—Geraldine	3455 Crestwood Dr., Beaumont, Tex.
2. George E. Watson	Ch. Mate	96264D1	Wf—Halga	6609 Golfcrest Dr., Galveston, Tex.
3. Henry P. Hall	2nd Mate	101668	Wf—Eunice	5270 Idylwood Beaumont, Tex.
4. Frank J. Cunningham	3rd Mate	236293D3	Wf—Angie	2366 Smart St. Beaumont, Tex.
5. George E. Sloat	Radio Off.	CDB29756	Wf—Monica	C/O ROU 20 E. Lexington St. Baltimore, Md.
6. Leon B. Clauser	Ch. Engr.	492924	Wf—Margaret	5350 Margo Lane Beaumont, Tex.
7. John L. Denton	1st Asst Eng	592836	Wf—Ann	Box 526 Friendswood, Tex.
8. A. R. Van Sickle	2nd Asst Eng	358646	Wf—June	2326 Grove St. Baltimore 30, Md.
9. E. W. Schneeberger	3rd Asst Eng	492842D2	Wf—Doris	Beaumont, Tex. 6650 Rebecca Lane

Name	Position	Z Number	Next of Kin	Address
10. Adam Martin	Jr. 3rd Asst Eng	476696	Wf—Edith	1105 W. 43rd St. Austin, Tex.
11. Evans Phillips	Bosun	618704	Wf—Thelma	4307 Suwanee Ave. Tampa, Fla.
12. Ceburn R. Cole	DM/AB	824413	Wf—Betty	Rte 4, Box 12 Lake Charles, La.
13. Jack R. Schindler	AB	213631	Sis—Mrs. J. Reed	2150 Fairmont, Seattle, Wash.
14. Fred A. Bodden	AB	1062351	Wf—Eva	1620 Lakecrest, Phila., Pa.
15. Everett E. Arnold	AB	270570D1	Sis—Virg. E. Hunt	1041 Gordon St. Memphis, Tenn.
16. Willie T. Manuel	AB	958644	Sis—Ena	Rt. 4, Box 92 Ville Platte, La.
17. James Mck. Bodden	AB	137516	Dau—Marina	4501 Webster St. Tampa, Fla.
18. Nelaton E. Devine	AB	294500D1	Mo—Kate	2203 11th St. Port Arthur, Tex.

Name	Position	Z Number	Next of Kin	Address
19. John M. Nieznajski	OS	315199D1	Sis—Ann Zachar	636 Carolina St. Gary, Ind.
20. Clarence Mcguire	OS	878339	Mo—Sarah	Bronsen, Tex.
21. James Phillips	OS	763291	Wf—Genoveva	428 Augusta Dr. Port Arthur, Tex.
22. Jessie I. Vicera	Pumpman	756487D1	Wf—Claire	120 E. Blancke St. Linden, N. J.
23. Alejandro Valdez	Oiler	804426	Wf—Josepha	1106 6th St. Port Arthur, Tex.
24. John C. Ardoin	Oiler	626542D1	Wf—Sally	3640 Youngstown St. Beaumont, Tex.
25. John Elmer Grice	Oiler	249208D2	Wf—Ethel	604 Van Ness St. Daytona Beach, Fla.
26. Henry Clark	FWT	317493D2	Bro—John	1106 Clairmont Ave. Jersey City, N.J.
27. Alphan Tate	FWT	1057668	Wf—Viola	705 Chestnut St. Phila., Pa.

Name	Position	Z Number	Next of Kin	Address
28. Leroy Courville	FWT	572043D1	Wf—Rena	5431 Hogaboom Rd. Groves, Tex.
29. John Husch, Jr.	Wiper	615290	Mo—Eliz.	1188 Cleveland-Mass Rd., Akron, Ohio
30. Aaron Heard	Wiper	1153038	Wf—Ada	816 Workwood Rd. Norfolk, Va.
31. Juan Santos	Wiper	10610D2	Wf—Josephine	12 Sheffield Dr. Newark, N. J.
32. Charles L. Dorsey	Ch. Stew.	339960D2	Wf—Ann	1415 Teller Ave. Bronx, N. Y.
33. Vincent Thompson	Ch. Cook	336028D1	Dau—Leona	406 Loudon Ave. Baltimore, Md.
34. Cornelius Smith	2nd Cook & Baker	105474	Wf—Hattie	1424 W. 7th St. Port Arthur, Tex.
35. Hugh D. Hunter	Galleyman	773083D1	Wf—Jimmie	605 Nunn St. Chapel Hill, N.C.
36. Walter Pleasant	Messman	1130682	Sis—Yvonne	612 E. 15th St. Port Arthur, Tex.

Name	Position	Z Number	Next of Kin	Address
37. Wesley Fontenot	Messman	805153D3	Mo—Enday	Mamou, La.
38. Robert E. Harold	Utilityman	551924D5	Sis—Vivian Price	610 Maltby Ave. Norfolk, Va.
39. Leroy B. Green	Utilityman	160065D2	Wf—Emma	1777 Newton St. Rahway, N. J.

Conclusion

1. The MARINE SULPHUR QUEEN disappeared on a voyage which commenced on 2 February from Beaumont, Texas and which was due to terminate on 7 February 1963 at Norfolk, Virginia. Since nothing was ever heard from the vessel after her departure, with the exception of the transmission of a personal message of a crew member, and further, in the light of the finding of scattered items of debris identified as coming from the vessel it is concluded that the MARINE SULPHUR QUEEN and her entire crew of 39 seamen must be presumed lost.

2. The evidence indicated that the vessel apparently encountered high winds and rough seas on 3 February while in the Gulf of Mexico and on 4 February while approaching the Straits of Florida. Further, the evidence shows that the vessel transmitted the personal radio message at 0125, EST on 4 February 1963 on behalf of a crew member and could not be contacted by the shore radio station commencing at 1123, EST, 4 February 1963. These facts in addition to the location of the scattered items of debris from the vessel would indicate that the vessel foundered some time on 4 February 1963 on the approach to or in the vicinity of the Straits of Florida.

3. In view of the absence of any survivors and the physical remains of the vessel, the exact cause for the disappearance of the MARINE SULPHUR QUEEN could not be ascertained.

4. In the absence of any evidence indicating a failure of the vessel's radio equipment, the failure to transmit a distress message would appear to justify the conclusion that the loss of the vessel occurred so rapidly as to preclude the transmission of such a message. On the other hand, the evidence does indicate that a few life jackets subsequently recovered appeared to have been worn by crew members. Under the cir-

175

cumstances, it is considered possible that these life jackets were worn by watch standers who had them readily available.

5. The board has considered many causes for the disappearance of the vessel. However, these causes remain only possibilities and the available evidence precludes the assignment of any order of probability to these causes. In the conclusions which follow no attempt is made to exhaust all possible causes for the vessel's disappearance. It is not the intent of the Board to negate the possibility that this casualty was occasioned by other causes which in the light of experience have been found to have resulted in the foundering of vessels.

6. Much evidence was received as to the general properties of molten sulphur and the gases formed in and liberated from this product with a view to assessing the possibility that the cargo contributed to the casualty. At the outset, it must be recognized that both grades of sulphur carried on this voyage were fairly pure with relatively small quantities of carbon impurities; the bright product containing .04% carbon and the dark .14% carbon. This fact would result in the formation of a smaller volume of gases than a product containing greater carbon impurities. Moreover, it appears that on this voyage the four cargo tanks were full into the trunks and that essentially the only air spaces in these tanks would be in the trunks themselves. Accordingly, it would appear that the total area of the spaces available for the collection of the gases was relatively small.

7. The evidence indicates that at least two explosive gases, namely hydrogen sulphide and carbon disulphide, are formed due to the reaction of the molten sulphur with organic matter normally contained in commercial sulphur. Although fairly soluble in the sulphur some of these gases are normally liberated from the mass of the sulphur. It is generally agreed, however, that agitation of the mass of the sulphur acts to increase the amount of the gases liberated from solution. It is concluded that the sulphur was agitated as the vessel worked in the rough seas which she apparently encountered on this voyage even though the tanks were fitted with swash bulkheads and were full into the expansion trunks. It, therefore, follows that this agitation of the molten sulphur increased the volume of these gases liberated from the molten sulphur.

176

8. Although each tank had one forward 6″ vent and two 4″ vents over the expansion trunks, the fact that all tanks had a full load of cargo on this voyage, being loaded into the trunks, prevented a free flow of air across the surface of the molten sulphur. Because of this, and the further circumstance that both hydrogen sulphide and carbon disulphide are heavier than air, it appears that on the instant voyage the venting arrangement was not too effective in clearing off these gases. Further, the evidence indicates that in rough weather, such as the vessel probably encountered on this voyage, the molten sulphur would pour out of the forward vents of the cargo tanks at least partially obstructing these vents as the sulphur solidified. If this condition existed on this voyage, it would further serve to impair the effectiveness of the venting arrangement.

9. The evidence further indicates that the auto-ignition point of carbon disulphide in concentrations within the flammability limits is 212°F. However, it appears that the other gas, hydrogen sulphide, having an auto-ignition point of 500° F, suppresses the carbon disulphide and acts to raise the auto-ignition point. Whether a layering of these gases can ever result has not been positively established. A study of the four reported explosions, made a part of the record of this Board, involving a barge, tank truck, storage tank and another ship all carrying or containing molten sulphur, fails to reveal the source of ignition of the gases. From all the evidence available, it is concluded that it could be possible that an explosion of the gases in the vapor space of one of the cargo tanks occurred. At the present state of knowledge, the source of ignition of such a possible explosion is only conjectural. The record contains tentative opinions of experts that the source of ignition of these explosions may be an electrostatic discharge, the presence of pyrophoric iron sulphide on the interior surfaces of the tanks, or the use of superheated steam in the heating coils. In this connection, it is to be noted that although a close inspection of the debris identified as coming from the vessel fails to show any evidence of charring or of an explosion, this fact by itself does not completely discount the possibility that an explosion did occur.

10. Although an explosion of the gases in one of the cargo tanks cannot be discounted, it would appear that such an explosion, if it occurred, would not be of a sufficient destructive force to account for the complete loss of the vessel without

177

the intervention of other causes, perhaps, resulting from the initial explosion. It seems to be a generally accepted fact that an explosion of these gases is, relatively speaking, and dependent upon the factors of quantity and space, not of a high order. This view is supported by the explosion which occurred on board a foreign flag T-2 type tanker converted to carry molten sulphur. In this case, despite a much larger air space, the explosion merely distorted the cargo tank without rupturing it. A consideration of other causes which may have been set in motion by a possible explosion of the gases in a cargo tank of the MARINE SULPHUR QUEEN would be purely conjectural. At this juncture it is pertinent to observe that the results of experiments being conducted by the Bureau of Mines into the properties of molten sulphur are not known and, accordingly, the present conclusions may have to be modified in the light of the results of these experiments.

11. Evidence has been received which indicates that on or before 29 April 1963 a note was found in a bottle on a spoil island in Laguna Madre off the Texas coast. This unsigned note purportedly written by a crew member speaks of two crew members being hurt as a result of an explosion. An examiner of questioned documents has stated his opinion that this note was written by a specified member of the crew on this voyage. On the other hand the Director of the Coast Geodetic Survey has stated that in his opinion the bottle could not have reached the site where it was found if dropped into the water at any place east of the 85th west meridian, unless a stong southeast wind was blowing for several days before and after the incident. The evidence indicates that on 3 and 4 February 1963 the wind was generally northerly. Also it would appear likely that the vessel had proceeded east of the 85th meridian before it foundered. Further, it is to be noted that all of the debris positively identified as coming from the vessel has been found off the southern tip of Florida. Finally, it is apparent that the preparation of this note, its insertion in the bottle, taping the bottle, and dropping it into the water must in all have consumed some considerable time. Without knowing all the facts existing at the time, it is difficult to explain why in this period of time, no radio distress message was transmitted from the vessel. For all these reasons, it is concluded that it is unlikely that this note was dropped into the water by a crew member of this vessel before it foundered.

12. The Board has extensively considered the possibility that the casualty to this vessel was caused by a complete longitudinal failure of the vessel's hull girder causing it to break in two. There are many factors bearing on this issue. Basically, insofar as this type vessel is concerned, the evidence indicates that there have been ten known cases of complete fractures of T-2 type tank vessels. That this type of casualty has persisted after the problem has been thoroughly studied and measures taken to prevent the same, tends to support the view held by some that this type of vessel has basic design imperfections which cannot be feasibly corrected. Additionally, it is now rather generally recognized, although previously a contrary view was held, that the age of a vessel has some relationship to structural failure. This instant vessel was about 17 years old at the time of the conversion and about 19 years old at the time of her disappearance.

13. As a result of her conversion, the center vertical keel of the MARINE SULPHUR QUEEN was cut down more than half its original height and deck centerline girder was cut down slightly less than half its height in the way of the cargo tanks. Further, one expert testified that in his opinion the slotted holes permitting the cargo tanks to expand were of an insufficient length and that even if of adequate length and properly aligned, the expansion of the tanks would add about 2,000 psi tensile stress to the hull. Also, the evidence indicates that on at least 52 loaded voyages of the 64 voyages made by this vessel after conversion, the sag numeral of 100 was somewhat exceeded, and that on the present voyage the sag numeral was 101.01 at the time of the vessel's departure from Beaumont. Finally, it appears the fairly rough seas which the vessel in all likelihood encountered on this instant voyage subjected the vessel to some longitudinal stress, despite the fact that it was essentially a beam sea.

14. On the other hand, the cutting down of the center vertical keel and the centerline deck girder was compensated for by adding substantial flange plates to these members and also by the construction of the cargo tank and its foundation. Calculations made after the conversion indicate that the section modulus of the vessel was increased about 2% in the deck and about 1% in the bottom as contrasted to the original section modulus. It is also to be noted that during conversion all the longitudinal deck girders in the way of the center tanks and many of these girders in the way of the wing tanks were

renewed. Finally, it is concluded that the excess of the sag numeral over 100 on the 52 voyages in question was so slight and that even the cumulative effect thereof would not appreciably affect the longitudinal strength of the vessel.

15. A major issue is whether or not the cargo tank was free to expand to the limits of its normal thermal expansion. This issue involves a consideration among other things of the adequacy of the length of the expansion slots in the longitudinal face plates. The evidence indicates that these slots were 3½ inches long except for the last ten feet on each end of the tank where the slots were 4 inches long. Mr. Rahe, the naval architect employed by the shipyard where the conversion took place, testified that his calculations and his inspection of the tank, after being heated by air to a temperature between 240° and 252° for 48 hours, indicated that the slots were of sufficient length. In this connection it is to be noted that no precise measurements of the actual expansion of the tank after this heated air test were made. Mr. Rahe, however, recalled that with respect to the slots near the ends of the tank, the bolts were between 3/8 of an inch to 1/4 of an inch from the end of the slots. Mr. Robertson, the Coast Guard naval architect, testified that his calculations indicated that some of these slots were not of adequate length.

16. The Board has made its own calculations of the thermal expansion of the tank on the assumption that there was proper alignment of the expansion slots and the bolts. These calculations are not conclusive primarily because of the difficulty in determining the correct figure to be used for the temperature differential. Theoretically, the temperature differential is determined by subtracting the average temperature of the metal of the tank at the time it was constructed and fitted in place from the highest temperature the metal of the tank attains in the actual service of carrying molten sulphur. It is noted that Mr. Rahe used a temperature differential of 200° F in his calculations on the assumption that the average temperature during the conversion work was 75° F and the highest temperature in service was 275° F. The temperature differential employed by Mr. Robertson appears to be 240° F.

17. Using a temperature differential of 200° F the Board calculations indicate that the slots were adequate in length provided proper alignment existed. However, using a temper-

ature differential of 240° F the Board calculations indicate the possibility that some slots, especially the 3½ inch slots nearest the ends of the tank, were inadequate even assuming proper alignment. Moreover, in view of the great number of slots and bolts involved, consideration must be given to the possibility that in fact there was not proper alignment of all these slots and bolts at the time of conversion.

18. According to the testimony of Mr. Rahe, which is confirmed by a study of the plans, no provision was made for the transverse and vertical thermal expansion of the tank on the assumption that these dimensions were small enough to permit the element of thermal expansion to be completely discounted. Were it not for this feature of the bolt and slot arrangement designed to take care of the longitudinal expansion, this assumption would probably be valid. However these bolts were 1 inch in diameter fitted in holes 1-1/16 inches in diameter and in slots 1-1/16 inches wide. Even the small amount of transverse and vertical thermal expansion would far exceed 1/16 of an inch and might well cause a binding of the bolts in the holes and slots.

19. On the other hand, the evidence does indicate that on every trip south after discharging the cargo the Chief Officer made an inspection of the void spaces with particular attention to the slots and bolts on the bottom of the tank. Furthermore, such an inspection was occasionally made by the port engineers employed by the operating company. The evidence unequivocally indicates that at no time were any sheared bolts found, nor was any binding of the bolts in the slots ever noted. However, even assuming these inspections were most thorough and competent, the results thereof do not affirmatively establish that the tank was in fact expanding freely to the limit of its normal thermal expansion. As a practical matter, this could only have been verified by a careful comparison of precise measurements of the actual expansion under controlled conditions with the calculations of thermal expansion at related points of the tank. This was in fact never done. Accordingly, when consideration is given to all these factors, it is concluded that it is possible that due to the inadequate length of some of the slots, the binding of the bolts in some of the slots due to transverse and vertical thermal expansion, the further binding of the bolts in some of the slots due to the motion of the vessel at sea, the lack of proper alignment, or a combination of these conditions, that

the tank was not expanding freely in a longitudinal direction to the limits of its normal thermal expansion. This possible loss of free movement to the degree that it was restricted would increase the compression stress of the tank and consequently the tension stress of the hull. Accordingly, on the basis of all the available evidence, it is concluded that it is possible that the casualty to the vessel originated with a complete longitudinal fracture of its hull girder. In reaching this conclusion the Board is not unmindful of the fact that in all previously known cases of a complete fracture of this type vessel, at least one section of the vessel has remained afloat. However, the conversion of this vessel significantly altered its basic characteristics and there is the further consideration that its cargo may have contributed to the rapid sinking of both sections, if in fact the vessel broke in two.

20. The evidence indicates that the vessel had a metacentric height in its loaded condition within the satisfactory range. However, the concentration of the weight of cargo within approximately 15 feet on either side of its centerline reduced the vessel's radius of gyration and, accordingly, its period of roll was faster than another vessel with the same metacentric height. The hindcast prepared by the U.S. Naval Oceanographic Office indicates the possibility that while the vessel was approaching the Straits of Florida it encountered seas with a maximum wave height of 16.5 feet slightly abaft its port beam. This hindcast further indicates the possibility that the period of encounter of the seas was within 10% of the vessel's period of roll, which was 8.5 seconds. Under these circumstances, heavy rolling of the vessel could be expected, accompanied by yawing, lurching and difficulty in steering. If such a situation developed, prompt appreciation of the danger by the watch officer and an immediate and drastic speed and/or course change would have been most vital. If complete resonance was approached, the vessel could have experienced several violent rolls in a minute's time. Accordingly, although no known reliable data is available to determine what the ultimate rolling of the vessel might have been, it is concluded that the possibility that the vessel capsized without previous structural damage cannot be discounted. Finally, it is possible that the capsizing of the vessel might have been preceded and caused in part by the partial failure of and some lateral displacement of the cargo tank due to the stresses previously and hereafter discussed.

21. The sea conditions which the vessel in all likelihood encountered on 3 and 4 February, also have a definite bearing on another possible cause for the vessel's disappearance. As a result of the conversion, nine transverse bulkheads in the way of the original center tanks were practically eliminated and the transverse web frames in the same area were cut down to accommodate the cargo tank. In the place of these original transverse strength members, one watertight bulkhead which completely surrounded the cargo tank was added at frame 59, two diaphragm bulkheads were added at frames 65 and 53 which connected merely the sides of the cargo tank with the longitudinal wing tank bulkheads, and top connections fitted with a bolt and slot arrangement were added at frames 71, 68, 62, 56, 50 and 47. In short, at the nine frames where originally there had been a watertight bulkhead in the amidship section of the vessel, after conversion there was one watertight bulkhead, two diaphragm bulkheads and six top connections. However, it is apparent that the replacement members did not possess the strength of the original watertight bulkheads. Moreover, the reduction in the height of the web frames was not completely compensated for by the addition of the flange plates. Therefore, it is concluded that the vessel after conversion did not possess the same transverse strength and stiffness as it had originally. Accordingly, it is considered possible that the moments induced by this racking may have contributed initially to cracking in the web frames or floors with displacement of the bottom structure and resulting cracking of the bottom shell. At the temperatures which reasonably could be expected at this time, the fractures up to this point could have been of the ductile slow type and could have occurred without causing noticeable sound or shock. As to what may have happened thereafter is conjectural. However, it is possible that this condition in turn brought into play other causes discussed herein which acting together may have produced the final major fracture of the vessel's hull. In this eventuality, it cannot be discounted that the foundering of the vessel could have occurred quite suddenly.

22. One factor which may have some relationship to the disappearance of the vessel could not be properly evaluated because of the lack of accurate information with respect thereto. This factor concerns the nature of the reaction resulting from the contact of large quantities of sea water and molten sulphur. As indicated by the Section 402 of the

NFPA Code No. 655 (1950), a Code for the Prevention of Sulphur Dust Explosion and Fires, there originally was some support for the view that the contact of these two liquids in a confined space would result in a steam explosion. However, the more recent thinking appears to discount the possibility of this reaction with the rationalization that the relatively cool sea water would quickly cool and solidify a layer of the sulphur which in turn would act to insulate the mass of the sulphur and the heat therein from further contact with the water. Nevertheless this later view does not completely discount the possibility of a steam explosion provided there is a rapid and very thorough dispersal and contact of the two liquids in a confined space. A related factor concerns the reaction resulting from the contact of sea water with the heated outside surfaces of the cargo tanks.

23. Both these factors may be of considerable significance in explaining the vessel's apparent sudden disappearance. One of the possible causes heretofore considered or some other cause may have resulted in sea water entering the void spaces surrounding the cargo tanks and coming into direct contact with the outside surfaces of the tanks, or with the sulphur itself, in the event of a rupture of a tank or tanks. Considering the state of the known knowledge on this subject a proper evaluation of these factors cannot presently be made. However, reference is again made to the experiments being conducted by the Bureau of Mines with the thought that the results of these experiments may permit a definitive evaluation of these factors to be made.

24. Considerable stress was placed during the investigation on the cause or causes for the several fires which occurred over a period of time in the void spaces surrounding the cargo tanks. The evidence does not permit any conclusions to be drawn as to the cause of these fires. It has been suggested that the spilled sulphur might have been ignited by coming into contact with short unlagged sections of the steam return lines from the heating coils at the bottom of the tanks. It has also been suggested that the auto-ignition temperature of sulphur may be reduced by the presence of contaminants and that the insulation surrounding the cargo tanks might be contaminated with oil or other organic materials reducing the auto-ignition temperature of the sulphur to the range of temperatures normally experienced on the outside of the cargo tanks. The inability to definitively establish the cause of these

known fires in the void spaces very cogently demonstrates the lack of complete and reliable information concerning all the properties of molten sulphur.

25. The plans for the conversion of the MARINE SULPHUR QUEEN to a molten sulphur carrier were prepared by a competent shipyard and were approved both by the American Bureau of Shipping and the U. S. Coast Guard. After the conversion the vessel was inspected and approved by these same agencies. Thereafter, both agencies inspected the vessel in October 1961 after she sustained heavy weather damage and approved the repairs made at that time. Subsequently both agencies inspected and approved the vessel in the early part of 1962 when she was subjected to a drydock and a Coast Guard mid-period inspection, and in January and February 1963 at which time the Coast Guard biennial inspection was held. Additionally, the vessel was inspected frequently by competent personnel serving on board and from time to time by port engineers and port captains employed by the operating company. The evidence indicates that after her conversion was commenced in 1960, all repairs required by the Americn Bureau and the Coast Guard were accomplished by the operating company within the allotted time. Further, there is no evidence to indicate that the operating company ever failed to make repairs requested or suggested by the Master. At the time of her disappearance the vessel had a valid certificate of inspection issued by the Coast Guard and was classified by the American Bureau of Shipping. On the basis of all this evidence, it is concluded that the operating company took all the customary precautions necessary to maintain a vessel associated with the carriage of petroleum products in a safe condition.

26. However, the MARINE SULPHUR QUEEN was not a conventional tanker carrying petroleum products. As a result of the conversion she was fitted with a fairly unique, massive, expanding tank and was carrying a cargo which up to that time had not been exclusively carried by a self-propelled vessel. It could, therefore, reasonably be expected that this new trade would involve new and unusual problems. Viewed against this background, the evidence indicates that the operating company failed to pursue good operating practice by not giving instructions or assistance to the Master of the vessel on many aspects of these problems and also failed to keep itself informed as to matters affecting the vessel's safety. In

general, the only instructions given to the Master of this vessel were the same as those given to a Master of a conventional tank vessel. Specifically, among other things, no instructions were given as to the method of loading and discharging cargo and the proper use of the Trim, Stability and Loading Booklet, safety procedures and tests to be observed during cargo operations, the temperature of the steam entering the heating coils, the temperature at which the cargo was to be maintained, tests of the cargo while at sea, the care and inspection of the venting systems to the cargo tanks and void spaces, inspection of the cargo tanks, void spaces and tank foundations, the temperature to be maintained on the empty cargo tanks, and the method and manner of ballasting the vessel. With respect to the failure to keep itself fully informed, it is significant that the operating company did not require a report from the Master as to the loading numerals for each voyage, despite the fact that this was required from all vessels which this same company operated on behalf of the Military Sea Transport Service. Further, it appears that while some of the personnel of the operating company had generally heard that a few fires had occurred in the void spaces, they were not fully informed as to all these fires and they never initiated any study in an attempt to determine the cause thereof. In summary, once the conversion was completed, except for a few minor details, the operating company treated this vessel as a conventional tank vessel. In so doing, it perhaps satisfied its responsibility under the law by permitting the duty for the safety of the vessel to devolve almost exclusively upon the Master. However, it is manifest that in handling exotic cargoes, of which molten sulphur is only one, that no mariner possesses the requisite expertise to solve all problems associated therewith. It is concluded that operating companies involved with such cargoes should thoroughly familiarize themselves with all the related problems and dangers involved, should if necessary seek outside expert advice, and should actively instruct and guide the Master in all aspects of handling the cargo and associated problems.

27. The operating company failed to give timely notice to the Coast Guard concerning the lack of communication from the vessel. The evidence indicates that the Master of the vessel had a reputation for punctuality in the transmission of arrival messages. The company rationalized the failure to receive the 48 hour and 24 hour arrival message on the basis of bad weather conditions and then delayed several hours

beyond the expected time of the vessel's arrival in Norfolk before notifying the Coast Guard. Needless to say, as a result of this delay, very valuable time was lost in instituting the search for the vessel and/or possible survivors.

28. The Coast Guard search for the missing vessel was most thorough and covered all possible areas in which the vessel could have been, if afloat, or in which debris and survivors could be reasonably expected, if sunk. The subsequent phase of search for the sunken vessel in the area of the Florida Straits, conducted by the United States Navy at the request of the Coast Guard, was most thorough and most unusual in its extent.

29. Relative to the approval of the conversion, the Merchant Marine Technical Division of Coast Guard Headquarters in its letter to Bethelem Steel Company dated 13 May 1960, while raising some issues as to the transverse strength of the vessel, approved the plans and specifications with the basic reservation that they be satisfactory to the American Bureau of Shipping and that compliance be had with all requirements of that society. This conditional approval by the Coast Guard is expressly authorized by the provisions of 46 CFR 31.10-1 (c). The evidence further indicates that the American Bureau of Shipping by its letter dated 21 June 1960 subsequently approved the conversion and the basic reservation of the Coast Guard approval was thus satisfied.

30. On the basis of hindsight, issue could be taken with the approval of the conversion of the vessel. However, in assessing these approvals, reference should be made only to the facts and information available at the time such approval was given. Furthermore, it must be borne in mind that the issue of the structural efficiency of a vessel's hull involves many imponderables and is not susceptible to precise and exact measurement. In the light of these considerations, it is concluded that no reason appears to question the approvals thus granted at that time. However, based on all the facts and information now available, the Board concludes that the same conversion of another T-2 type tanker should not be approved at this time, nor should any other conversion be approved that deviates from the originally designed features or the carriage of the basic petroleum products.

31. The evidence indicates that during the course of the ves-

sel's mid-period inspection in 1962 and the biennial inspection in 1963, the Coast Guard marine inspectors, although conducting, in general, a very thorough and conscientious inspection of the vessel, failed to make a sufficiently detailed inspection of the cargo tanks, tank fittings and surrounding void areas. This failure appears to have been primarily attributable to unfamiliarity on the part of the inspectors with the basic designed cargo tank arrangements of the vessel and the properties of the cargo that she carried. It would appear that the Coast Guard inspectors proceeded on the assumption that the MARINE SULPHUR QUEEN was a conventional tanker fitted for the carriage of "Grade E cargoes" with certain relaxations permitted by 46 CFR, Part 36. Even though the evidence indicates that inspection of the cargo tank, fittings and surrounding void areas were made periodically by vessel and company personnel, a more careful inspection of these members and spaces should have been made by the Coast Guard inspectors to adequately assess the condition of the vessel.

32. Viewed realistically the responsiblity for this failure cannot be placed exclusively on the inspectors themselves or their immediate commanding officer. They were summoned to conduct inspections of this vessel without any intimation that this vessel was not merely a conventional tanker modified for "Grade E cargoes" and without being informed that the vessel had a unique cargo arrangement which required close scrutiny. In the future, it would appear preferable to treat vessels of this type as unique vessels rather than as modified conventional tankers. Moreover, with respect to these unique vessels, which apparently will become more numerous in the future, consideration should be given by the Commandant to the establishment of procedures to insure that field officers in their inspection of these vessels place greater emphasis on the safety of the cargo and the related design features.

Recommendations

1. In the future, the same conversion of another T-2 type tanker should not be approved. Further, it is recommended that no other conversion of this type vessel should be approved which deviates from the originally designed features for the carriage of normal petroleum products.

2. Molten sulphur carriers should be required to install a device to automatically record the temperature of the steam entering the heating coils, together with an automatic alarm in the event of abnormal temperatures.

3. The void space surrounding molten sulphur cargo tanks should be required to be fitted with appropriate fire hose stations.

4. Appropriate portable instrument manufacturers should be advised of the need for a suitable explosimeter that will accurately measure the explosive gases emanating from molten sulphur in order that frequent checks of the gas content in a tank can be required to be made by ship's personnel.

5. The companies operating molten sulphur carriers should be required to provide appropriate instructions to and indoctrinate all vessel personnel in the hazards of molten sulphur. This indoctrination should include the dangers of agitation occurring during loading and while the vessel is at sea.

6. The final results of the experiments being conducted by the Bureau of Mines into the chemical and/or physical properties of molten sulphur should be carefully studied by the Commandant with a view to assessing their impact on all vessels approved by the Coast Guard for the carriage of such cargo.

7. With respect to vessels of unique design handling exotic

cargoes, consideration should be given by the Commandant to the establishment of procedures to insure that the Coast Guard field inspection officers are informed, in advance of the actual inspection, as to the essential cargo features of these vessels and the significant areas of inspection. It is further recommended that these procedures require a full report of the completed inspection to be submitted by the field inspection office to the Commandant.

8. In the future when Coast Guard approval of a vessel designed to carry exotic cargoes is sought, the company seeking the approval should be required to submit reasonable studies acceptable to the Commandant of all the chemical and/or physical properties of these cargoes and, when necessary, such properties should be given full consideration in the design of the vessel. Further, the Commandant with the assistance of the Chemical Transportation Panel to the Merchant Marine Council should establish minimum criteria for these studies to be submitted by the company seeking the approval.

9. During the conduct of this investigation it was quite apparent from the testimony before the Board that there were many problem areas concerning the transportation of molten sulphur which to date are unresolved. These areas, among others, concern: (1) shape, size and attachment of cargo tanks, (2) ventilation of cargo tanks, (3) thermal expansion, (4) evolution and release of gases, and (5) the auto-ignition point of molten sulphur when in contact with insulating materials. Since molten sulphur is essentially an exotic cargo, it is recommended that the requirements of recommendation 8 above should be met before any new or converted construction is approved by the Coast Guard. Further, in the case of existing vessels engaged in the carriage of molten sulphur, the Commandant should have a study made as to any hazards to personnel or the ships themselves which may have existed. If such study indicates the present existence of such hazards, it is recommended that the Commandant take appropriate action.

10. Consideration should be given to the establishment of procedures, preferably voluntary, which will provide the owner, agent, or operating companies of all vessels of the United States, engaged in foreign or coastwise voyages, with a daily position report of these vessels.

11. Consideration should be given to the implementation at the earliest practicable date of the provisions of Recommendation 48 of the International Convention for the Safety of Life at Sea, 1960, concerning the carriage of an Emergency Position-Indicating Radio Beacon, which would automatically transmit a distress signal in the event of the sinking of a vessel.

12. In view of the complete structural failures of several T-2 type tank vessels, and in view of the fact that such type failure may have contributed to the instant casualty, it is recommended that with respect to all tankers of 3,000 gross tons and upwards on which lifeboats are fitted amidships and aft, that consideration be given to the implementation at the earliest practicable date of the provision of Chapter III, Regulation 13, of the International Convention for the Safety of Life at Sea, 1960, requiring a portable emergency radio transmitter to be kept in a suitable place in the vicinity of the after lifeboats. For the same reasons, it is also recommended that consideration be given by the Commandant to the establishment of a requirement that all T-2 type tank vessels be equipped with two inflatable life rafts, one to be located in the vicinity of the forward deckhouse and the other to be located in the vicinity of the afterhouse.

Selected Bibliography

Berlitz, Charles, *The Bermuda Triangle*. New York, Doubleday & Co., 1974.

Burgess, Robert F., *Sinkings, Salvages, and Shipwrecks*. New York, American Heritage Press, 1970.

Gaddis, Vincent, *Invisible Horizons*. Philadelphia, Chilton Books, 1965.

Gould, Rupert, *Enigmas*. New Hyde Park, N.Y., University Books, 1965.

Hoehling, A. A., *They Sailed into Oblivion*. Cranbury, N.J., Thomas Yoseloff & Co., 1958.

Kusche, Lawrence David, *The Bermuda Triangle Mystery— Solved*. New York, Harper & Row, 1975.

Sanderson, Ivan T., *Invisible Residents*. New York, World Publishing Co., 1970.

Spencer, John Wallace, *Limbo of the Lost*. Westfield, Mass., Phillips Publishing Co., 1969.

Villiers, Alan, *Wild Ocean*. New York, McGraw-Hill, 1957.

Winer, Richard, *The Devil's Triangle*. New York, Bantam Books, 1974.

About the Editor

Martin Ebon served for twelve years as Administrative Secretary of the Parapsychology Foundation and subsequently as a consultant to the Foundation for the Study of the Nature of Man. He has conducted a series of lectures on "Parapsychology: From Magic to Science" at the New School for Social Research in New York. He has edited such periodicals as the quarterly *Tomorrow*, the scholarly *International Journal of Parapsychology,* and *Spiritual Frontiers,* organ of the Spiritual Frontiers Fellowship.

Mr. Ebon has contributed articles and reviews to a variety of periodicals, ranging from *Saturday Review* to the U.S. Naval Institute *Proceedings*. He has written over fifteen books for NAL alone. Among his books are EXORCISM: FACT NOT FICTION, THE PSYCHIC SCENE, and TRUE EXPERIENCES IN PROPHECY.

Other SIGNET Titles You'll Want to Read

☐ **THE ULTIMATE ELSEWHERE by J. H. Brennan.** There is an invisible world around you at this very moment! All over the world, people disappear in the blink of an eye, some never to be seen again, others to return with amazing stories of what they have seen and heard. Now at last a book moves through the centuries and around the globe to piece together the age-old mysteries that have haunted man since the beginning of time. . . .
(#W6463—$1.50)

☐ **UFOs . . . AND THEIR MISSION IMPOSSIBLE by Dr. Clifford Wilson, M.A., B.D., Ph.D.** What Chariots of the Gods? did not tell you! The first book to reveal the purpose of the UFOs and what we can do to head off the danger threatening earth and its inhabitants.
(#W6424—$1.50)

☐ **ALIENS FROM SPACE . . . THE REAL STORY OF UN-IDENTIFIED FLYING OBJECTS by Major Donald E. Keyhoe (USMC Ret.).** From secret Washington archives, eyewitness testimonies and official scientific findings, new astounding evidence about Von Daniken's ancient astronauts and their landings on Earth today!
(#W6206—$1.50)

☐ **GODS AND SPACEMEN OF THE ANCIENT PAST by W. Raymond Drake.** Does the blood of ancient spacemen flow in your veins? Here are all the pieces of the jigsaw puzzle that reveals for the first time how beings from space once dominated Earth, and not only ruled but actually mated with its people. Here is the startling evidence about the siege of Troy, the ancestry of Alexander the Great and Jesus, the raising of the Pyramids, and much, much more. Here is the boldest yet the most convincing book you have ever read!
(#W6140—$1.50)

THE NEW AMERICAN LIBRARY, INC.,
P.O. Box 999, Bergenfield, New Jersey 07621

Please send me the SIGNET BOOKS I have checked above. I am enclosing $_____(check or money order—no currency or C.O.D.'s). Please include the list price plus 25¢ a copy to cover handling and mailing costs. (Prices and numbers are subject to change without notice.)

Name_____

Address_____

City_____State_____Zip Code_____
Allow at least 3 weeks for delivery